From the Heart of Europe
Anthology of Contemporary Slovenian Writing

*t*P
Texture Press

From the Heart of Europe

Anthology of Contemporary Slovenian Writing

Introduction by
MATEJ BOGATAJ

Translated from the Slovene by
Tamara Soban, Erica Johnson Debeljak, Evald Flisar, Lili Potpara,
Gerald Hansen, Maja Novak, Sonja Kravanja, Rawley Grau

TEXTURE PRESS
Guilderland, New York
Norman, Oklahoma

Published by Texture Press
Guilderland, New York
Norman, Oklahoma
texturepress@beyondutopia.com
First printing, September 2007

ACKNOWLEDGEMENTS: The publisher gratefully acknowledges
the financial assistance of Trubar Foundation.

Library of Congress Cataloging-in-Publication Data

From the Heart of Europe
Anthology of contemporary Slovenian prose / edited by Evald Flisar.
    p. cm.
    ISBN 978-0-9712061-8-2

    1.Slovenian prose literature – 20th century. I. Flisar, Evald.
    PG1916.A57 2007
    891.8'4608–dc22
    2007021240

PRINTED IN THE UNITED STATES OF AMERICA
Set in Times New Roman
Cover design by Sanja Jansa

PUBLISHER'S NOTE
These stories are works of fiction. Names, characters, places, and incidents
either are the product of the author's imagination or are used fictitiously,
and any resemblance to actual persons, living or dead, events, or locales in
entirely coincidental.

CONTENTS

CONTEMPORARY SLOVENIAN LITERATURE:
A Cohabitation, in Principle, of Styles and Generations

Matej Bogataj

1. The Birth of a Nation

In 2000, as we entered a new millennium, cultural attention in Slovenia focused on the celebration of the bicentennial of the birth of the foremost and greatest Slovenian poet, France Prešeren, the founder and epitome of Slovenian romantic poetry; he introduced a number of poetic forms into the Slovenian language, and honed to perfection the Petrarchan sonnet. The year-long festivities, which included many public readings of Prešeren's poetry, were by no means just another incidental project to expand the annual celebration of the national cultural holiday on the day of the poet's death, or to rekindle interest in or uphold the literary tradition. On the contrary, Prešeren and literature in general form the foundation of Slovenian national identity. The attention bestowed on Prešeren more than 150 years after his death is not attention paid to poetry as a literary form, but derives from the awareness that

7

the significance of Prešeren's and all subsequent poetry far surpasses its literary importance.

One of the greatest Slovenian thinkers of the 20th century, the philosopher and literary historian Dušan Pirjevec, wrote in his brilliant study from the mid-1970s about our reception of poetry that literature was a privileged and representative field for the articulation of the Slovenian national interest owing also to the fact that few Slovenian scientists had ever worked in Slovenia, that there had been practically no successful Slovenian generals, in particular not in a national, Slovenian army, while the politicians had been doomed to pragmatism and compromise. With the exception of the first writings in Slovenian, Brižinski spomeniki (The Freising Fragments) from the 9th century, literature did more than serve merely as a tool for preserving the language as a basis for national identity: it was also a vehicle of protest against desperate circumstances and a promise of a brighter future. Like the mythological Orpheus, a poet is literature's supreme organ upon whom the power has been bestowed to foretell the future and unite people into a community. Few nations can – like the Slovenians – claim without irony to have arisen and been preserved thanks to poetic visions.

Prešeren's "Zdravljica" ("A Toast"), more than 150 years old, technically a drinking-song, that is to say an easygoing, merry poem – and since the declaration of independence and sovereignty in the 1990s also the Slovenian national anthem – already contains allusions to the notion of the Slovenians united as a nation equal to other European nations, integrated in a community now known as the European Union. Not long ago Slovenia joined the Union as a full member.

The verses from the anthem "Let's drink that every nation/ Will live to see that bright day's birth/ When 'neath the sun's rotation/ Dissent is banished from the earth,/ All will be/ Kinfolk free/ With neighbours none in enmity"* were in the first half of the 19th century above all utopian, but at the same time also politically provocative enough to be censored and banned in the Austro-Hungarian empire. That the vision has nevertheless come true is above all due to the belief of the most far-sighted thinkers of all the generations since then.

2. Waiting for Statehood

With the exception of the Carantania period in the 6th century, when our ancestors voted for and instated their own princes in a manner similar to that followed by Thomas Jefferson in writing the Declaration of Independence, Slovenians were politically not sovereign. This implied a position in a strategically vulnerable part of Europe, exposed to Turkish invasions and the encroachment of Islam, and consequently particularly fragile and sensitive to the Germanic and Romance influences which converged in this part of Europe. Slovenians were divided between several countries, often involved in hostilities; during the First World War, one of the most important and bloody frontlines ran along the Soča (Isonzo) River valley, with conscripted Slovenian soldiers fighting on both sides. After the end of the First World War, Slovenians joined Serbians, Croatians, Macedonians and other southern Slav peoples to form the kingdom of Yugoslavia, which transformed into a socialist republic after the Second World War and ultimately disintegrated in the 1990s, a decade after the death of the dictator Josip Broz Tito, its leader since the end of the Second World War. The 1990s were a time of *perestroika* and of countries formerly part of the Soviet Union gaining independence,

* Translated from the Slovenian by Tom Priestly and Henry Cooper

9

which unquestionably also reduced and weakened the position of the centralist forces in Yugoslavia, i.e., the hardened communist core which took the side of Serbian chauvinism. Subsequent to the Memorandum of the Serbian Academicians, which demanded that all Serbians be united within one state, and the coming to power of Slobodan Milošević, there followed a change of the Yugoslavian constitution which deprived the Albanians in Kosovo of their autonomy. Although the Albanians represented over 90 percent of the population in the autonomous province of Kosovo, they were denied their political rights and, when they protested, their basic human rights were violated. The other republics faced a long, painful and often unproductive process of asserting their interests, which after many unsuccessful talks and attempts to protect human rights ended with declarations of independence on the part of Slovenia and Croatia. The federal army intervened; there followed a brief, ten-day war in Slovenia, after which Slovenia was recognized as a sovereign state. The later grisly ethnical clashes in Croatia, Bosnia and Kosovo revealed the depth and strength of interethnic hatred and chauvinism in the region, which had simmered unabated all the time just beneath the surface of communist internationalism, and now acquired bestial proportions.

3. Mythology and Literature

The absence of political sovereignty demanded a great deal of pragmatism and suspended decision-making if the Slovenians were to survive as a nation, as is also apparent in the repressed character of the great Slovenian myths. To this day they remain subject to various adaptations and interpretations, which clearly indicates that the myths still present a challenge for our sense of self-understanding and justification. They all point to a fundamental inactivity, or inability to act, reflecting the unbearable plight into which the central characters are forced.

The myth of Črtomir, the defeated Slovenian pagan warlord, who embraces Christian faith out of love for his already Christianised beloved and goes off to convert his people, is in general the most frequently exploited motif in contemporary Slovenian literature, even in the work of the present-day generation of authors. A possible explanation for its (continued) topicality would seem to be the fact that it is open-ended and has conversion as its main theme.

Generally speaking, mythology, also classical, is frequent in post-war drama, in particular in poetic drama; its creator during modernism was Ivan Cankar, who combined various *fin-de-siècle* trends, symbolism, new romanticism, neo-naturalism. Some of the most prominent Slovenian post-war dramatists and poets also wrote poetic dramas, which were basically poetic language spun around the frame of a myth or mythological story: Dane Zajc, Gregor Strniša, Veno Taufer, and also Ivo Svetina. The use of language and choice of topic differ to a certain extent in the works of authors representative of the so-called political drama, Rudi Šeligo, Dušan Jovanović, and Drago Jančar. The theatre has always been a degree more political than other literary forms, therefore it is not surprising that in the mid-1970s there existed a very strong branch of socially involved drama which nevertheless preserved a high level of linguistic articulation. Dominik Smole's adaptation of Sophocles' *Antigone*, in which the title character does not even make an appearance, is unquestionably the most salient and paradigmatic work of this genre. It is about a soldier killed in a civil war while fighting for the defeated side, and consequently denied the right to burial, which is in conflict with the timeless law of burying the dead. In this, *Antigone* alludes to the events in recent Slovenian history; exacting an incredibly cruel revenge, the winning side executed over ten thousand people after the end of the Second World War. The Communist Party – which during the national liberation struggle against the Nazi occupying forces gradually carried out a social revolution and after the war instated a one-party political system – made any discussion of this particular or all other errors and instances of self-will impossible, and also generally thwarted any attempts at oppositional political activities. Authors and literary interpreters who gathered around such prominent literary magazines as *Beseda*, *Perspektive* and *Revija 57* were the only ones to broach the forbidden subjects, thus embodying the important voices of social conscience. They were often persecuted for their efforts, some of them even incarcerated and their books banned, while the magazines were discontinued. Despite all this there were few real dissidents in the sense known in Eastern Europe, since the Yugoslavian regime was much more permissive than those in Eastern European countries, placed somehow "in between" East and West. This was primarily a consequence of 1948, when Tito and the communist leadership decided to stand up to Stalinism. All this notwithstanding, we cannot speak of any degree of democracy until the mid-1970s, since all political activities were prevented, while cultural activities were strictly controlled and in the cases of transgression subjected to political threats.

Only in the light of the absence of political pluralism can the importance of certain post-war poetic phenomena be understood and evaluated, including those which spoke of existential angst, of intimate emotions, without explicitly referring to social reality; writing was per se oppositional in its role and significance, because it represented the only medium of truth, even when its purpose was primarily literary. Poets and authors were among the first to voice demands for the democratization of the society and, as soon as this became possible, themselves formed and headed political parties. Some of them have remained in politics, participating in the writing of the constitution and similar activities, some have returned to writing, and some got stuck half-way and are politically active behind the scenes. But even today, with the achieved level of democracy, the notion is still alive that writers' organizations and magazines should take a more active role in political life; it is, however, true that the activities of the civil society petered out as the various party politics polarized, and what now calls itself the 'civil initiative' is often just a front for airing badly disguised party views. Occasionally, writers too get caught up in endorsing or opposing individual institutional changes, but the real casualty of the decline in general solidarity is their primary field, literature. Literature is increasingly the target of neoliberal pressures, which started as newspaper pamphlets and demagogy and have now taken the form of concrete actions by bureaucrats and their political godfathers. What is sorely lacking is a unified, consensual stand taken by the writers' organizations to give their unanimous support to the future development of publishing, to preventing the gradual erosion of authors' fees, to promoting the distribution of literature, to opposing the high taxation of books, and similar issues. Otherwise, writers could end up having even less say in decisions regarding their own professional field and, consequently, their organizations could break up. As the space to maneuver shrinks, the notion unfortunately seems to be surfacing that only some will survive; so now a part of the community of writers is jostling to ensure their survival, of course, at the expense of all those kept at bay. Incidentally, Slovenia is one of the few countries of transition – if not the only one – that still has a single writers' society, The Slovenian Writers' Association; elsewhere, the divisions and discord were so profound that parallel organizations were established, based primarily on political views.

13

4. Opening up to the World

Today Slovenia is a country of 20,000 square kilometers, with a population of approximately 2 million, ranking highest among the lower half of European Union countries in terms of economic development; it has completed the process of transition, i.e., the transformation of socially-owned property into private property, and has in this respect been, apparently, one of the most successful new member countries, and also the first to adopt euro as the national currency. The decision in favor of the European integration processes seems to be consensual. There was more reluctance regarding Slovenia's membership in the military organization NATO, which intensified when Slovenia started sending Slovenian soldiers off to wars that began with false allegations of reasons for intervention, such as the war in Iraq.

Slovenian statehood has altered the role of literature to a certain degree; after the profound interest in literature which peaked in the 1980s, when attending a literary reading often had a political connotation and expressed support for the demands for the democratic transformation of the society, achievements in other domains, like the economy, sports and sciences, have also become significant for the identity of the Slovenians, not to mention the activities of the Slovenian members of the European parliament and other political and cultural institutions of the new union of nations. This has enabled literature to turn back to itself, to its own procedures, and as a result the interest in it has flagged; literature is currently losing its privileged position to other media, particularly the visual ones. In a similar way to other, larger European nations, Slovenia is awakening to the reality that the national and regional specific features need to be protected from disappearing in the global melting pot of the penetrating world entertainment

14

industry. A defensive stance focusing only on national identity can of course be dangerous and lead to a hermetic and self-sufficient culture, a thing that has not happened in the past. The cultural flow in this part of Europe has always been very strong; ever since the Enlightenment, all European literary trends have reverberated in the works of Slovenian artists who produced first-rate works. There exist Slovenian translations of virtually all the crucial works of the major European and Anglo-American literatures; we have a considerably detailed insight into smaller national literatures; contacts with the countries of the former Yugoslavia are being renewed; and literary magazines follow closely all that is new anywhere in the world.

There are also many institutionalized international exchanges. The post-war PEN congresses in Bled, in which numerous world-renowned literary guests took part, were among the first to host authors from both East and West, which was possible only in Slovenia as a space in-between. The PEN played a very important part later on as well, with its reflections on the carnage in the Balkans, with the discussions always broaching the most problematic subjects and having far-reaching echoes. One of the merits of the Slovenian PEN is that it has called attention to the humanitarian needs of all the victims of the war on the territory of Yugoslavia and openly pointed to the crimes deliberately perpetrated in the name of ethnic cleansing.

Extensive exchanges take place between Slovenian and foreign literary magazines, encompassing all literary generations. The Slovenian Writers' Association issues a periodic publication *Litterae Slovenicae,* which presents the most representative Slovenian authors in translations into major foreign languages in order to give at least a rough idea of their work and arouse further interest. The Slovenian Writers' Association is the founder and organizer of the annual international convention at Vilenica, where every year an award is presented to a prominent European author, while during the debate the authors and essayists address the most pressing problems in Central Europe. The Vilenica festival was also founded with the objective of emphasizing Slovenia's long-standing alliance with Central European culture and establish the characteristics and differences of the region. The main activity of the Center for Slovenian Literature is international cooperation; so far, the Center has organized and coordinated several important tours by Slovenian authors abroad, in particular in countries with which Slovenia has not yet established channels of exchange.

The goal of the National Program for Culture, adopted in 2000, is to unite the more or less scattered funds and institutions involved in the international exchange of artistic production into a single body: the Trubar Foundation, named for the author of the first books in Slovenian, a Protestant who had to leave his homeland during the Counter-Reformation and work in Germany. Both directly and on the basis of international exchange and bilateral agreements, the Foundation tries to increase the extent and ensure the highest possible quality of the presentation of Slovenian authors abroad and compile a clear and integral database. A two-million strong nation must take an active part in cultural trends if it is to survive and preserve its right to being different. We can take courage from the fact that, parallel to globalization, the reverse process is also in progress, nurturing specificity and difference, focusing on local and regional traits. The National Program for Culture aims to establish a model of cultural life which would enable valuable marginal phenomena to survive and at the same time create the conditions for the best possible achievements in art. What is problematic is that a strategic document about culture is just a piece of paper, a load of empty promises, unless backed by a concrete policy with specific numbers. Despite the optimism repeatedly expressed by whatever political option is in power, the fact remains that the position of the Slovenian book is deteriorating, that authors' fees are being reduced, that the conditions for acquiring the official status of a person self-employed in the field of culture are increasingly hard to meet, that smaller publishing houses are exposed to greater pressures and find it harder and harder to transfer funds from commercial programs to publications of original literature, while an institution with the decisive role in international exchange could easily favor "its own" authors, i.e., those inclined to the political option momentarily in power. Due to its small size, Slovenia is even more vulnerable to underhand deals with privileges and loyalty than other countries.

5. Publishing

Despite the redistribution of capital, widespread sponsoring of art is not yet an established practice in Slovenia, with the exception of a small number of big corporations which, however, are finding the taxation system adverse to this type of investment. As a result, sometimes absurd situations occur: a sponsor finances, say, a theatrical production but refuses to be named as the sponsor lest some overzealous taxman – and there is no shortage of those – charges them with unearmarked expenditure of funds. This is primitive neoliberalism on the go. The main source of funding for publications of original Slovenian literature thus remains the national budget, distributed by the relevant Ministry and its committees.

Today there are approximately 150 publishing houses in Slovenia, which annually bring out about 4500 titles. Due to the smallness of the literary market, original Slovenian literature – with very few exceptions – cannot appear in editions which could cover the costs of authors' fees and printing. For this reason the state subsidizes about 250 titles per year, more than half of which are original Slovenian literary works, while the rest are scientific studies and essays. For the subsidized books, the state bears most of the publishing costs; the publishers need to cover less than half with the sale of the books, but are obliged to pay fees fixed by the state – which they don't – and are restricted in setting the price. Subsidies increase the number of books published and ensure reader-friendly prices, thus boosting the accessibility of books.

It was characteristic of the 1980s that small, penetrating publishing houses temporarily took the initiative; however, they have been unable to survive, due to inadequate or difficult distribution and small editions (collections of verse sell on the average 500 copies, and novels up to 1000 copies). There are still numerous non-profit publishing houses and book collections published by literary magazines, which seems to indicate that the state is, despite the growing adversity, still relatively responsive to such initiatives. But also the reverse, basically negative trend is present in Slovenian publishing: a segment of capital, originating from wild privatization, took over virtually all the major publishing houses without possessing a vision for their future activities, and then sold them on to its main competitor, which thus became, for all intents and purposes, a monopolist, and commensurately unconcerned with its public image and arrogant toward original Slovenian literature.

The relatively small editions do not mean that the reading culture in Slovenia is not highly developed: one of the key ways in which books – in particular original Slovenian literature and translated works – reach their readers is through public libraries. There exists a dense network of libraries which are virtually free of charge and open to the general public, and all are obliged to buy works of original Slovenian literature;

18

thus successful Slovenian authors are well known to the reading public.

The state also financially supports approximately 70 cultural and scientific magazines. The best known are teeming centers of literary life; *Nova revija*, *Literatura* and *Sodobnost*, and increasingly also *Apokalipsa* and its book collection, represent different orientations. *Nova revija* unites between its covers predominantly the modernist generation, which established itself on the literary scene in the 1960s and then became, together with its theoretical companions, most actively involved in the process of democratization; its theoretical background is primarily Heidegger's philosophy and phenomenology, and its literary trend, modernism and its offshoots, gradually less radical. *Literatura* unites those who began writing in the 1980s and 1990s and are often classified as postmodernist, despite their diverse literary approaches. Until 1998, *Sodobnost*, one of the four oldest European literary magazines, hosted predominantly traditional writers, but has now opened up to the younger generations and been invigorated by new blood, becoming a truly contemporary, globally orientated journal. Generally speaking, one of the main characteristics of Slovenian literary life seems to be a considerable degree of mutual tolerance between and co-habitation of diverse literary practices; rather than being competitive and exclusive, literary trends intertwine and coexist, sometimes even merge, though rather on the basis of quite pragmatic, financial effects than of esthetic criteria, especially when it comes to flirting with the number one sponsor, the Ministry of Culture. Of course, literary magazines need at the same time to cultivate their specific identities and seek out phenomena at home and abroad with which to underscore them. We believe that the literary climate in Slovenia is favorable and productive, although the relatively good times are not getting better, and may be getting worse –

which is most apparent in the increased pressures on the small publishing houses and in the harsher conditions for those applying for the status of a person self-employed in the field of culture. In spite of this, representative works of art are being created here, which we gladly offer to the world to read.

Hopefully, this selection will serve as an incentive to search for further information on Slovenian literature; only a more detailed presentation can portray all of its variety and diversity.

Translated by Tamara Soban

Andrej Blatnik

Andrej Blatnik *(Ljubljana, 1963) played bass guitar in a punk band and studied a great many things, finishing with a PhD in Communication Studies. At present, he earns his living as editor and part-time teacher of creative writing. Andrej has published two novels, four collections of short stories, and three books of essays in Slovenian, as well as fourteen books in other languages including Spanish (Cambios de piel, Libertarias/Prodhufi 1997), Croatian, English (Skinswaps, Northwestern University Press 1998), Czech, Hungarian, Slovakian, French, Macedonian and German (Der Tag, an dem Tito starb, Folio, 2005). He has read his short stories around the globe and received various fellowships, including Fulbright, and various literary awards. He enjoys traveling, always on a shoestring. A list of his publications, along with some samples, is available at www.andrejblatnik.com.*

ELECTRIC GUITAR

Andrej Blatnik

Hidden in the dusk, the boy tries over and over to pick out that miserable tune on the accordion. He can't do it. Not a single note forms a harmony with its predecessor; his fingers on the buttons sometimes reach too low, then too high, and every time the bellows bleat out a jarring discord. The boy is not very musical, but he knows enough to realize that his goal – to play the simple air correctly – is becoming increasingly unattainable with every passing moment, just as the time when his father will return, and demand to be played to, is drawing inexorably nearer.

The night descends upon him like a damp cloth. The dense clusters of music printed on the sheet first begin to blend, then disappear altogether in the dark. The boy does not turn on the light since the dark brings relief; it is awful to watch one's fingers stumbling over one another in helpless confusion on the keys.

Now he can only hear them. He does not hear the awkward elusive melody, only his own fingers refusing obedience. And he knows that once again he won't be able to make his father see that it's not his fault, it's his fingers that are to blame. The more he'll explain how hard he's tried to unravel the mystery of this tune, the more entangled he'll get and the clearer it'll become that in actual fact he still doesn't know for certain what some of the symbols on the music sheets mean and that every now and then he leaves out a couple. His father will hear him out patiently, as he always does, while at the same time he'll already be pulling the belt out of his pants. And then he'll say: Go on, son, play it again.

And the boy will play it again and the tune will be even more jagged as his fingers leave sweat marks on the keys, making them slippery. And the father will listen and stroke his leather belt, and then he'll say: Son, put away the accordion.

The boy thinks about what is to come and tears well up in his eyes. The worst part is that he loves music. When he lies in bed at night, he shuts his eyes tight and imagines himself as that boy in a white tuxedo and bow tie he'd seen on television, standing center stage in a concert hall, holding a violin in his hand and taking a bow while the audience applauded enthusiastically. His reality is different: His only audience is his father, and he doesn't clap for joy.

The boy knows what is wrong, he knows why he can't find the right notes. He's under the spell of the electric guitar. It's everywhere. It's got all the right sounds and won't let his accordion have a single one of them. It's gone to his head and filled it with a white buzz that doesn't allow any rivals near. That's why his quaking tones can't flow together into a melody. They're not allowed to by the electric guitar. The one that always finds the way. He saw that on television too. He saw how it had all started. Somewhere far away, somewhere in Africa, the devil played the guitar and cast such a spell on it that nobody but its owner could play it. Everyone else was struck by a bolt. Burned to ashes. Made them be no more. And that's why guitars are so dangerous. And the electric guitar, the most powerful of them all, is the most dangerous. If you're not the right person for it, that is.

24

The boy thinks: If I had an electric guitar, a real one, then I could do it. He'd be the right person for it and he could play it without a miss, and his father would not take the belt out of his pants, but would open his arms and lift him up and tell him how proud he was of him and the audience would clap their hands and he would adjust his bow tie, press the violin against his white tux and leave the stage and go back to his room where the two toys would be waiting for him, the toys on which the dust settles relentlessly during the hours when he so desperately tries to find the right line over the black and white keys. And then he would put the violin away and play with them, the teddy bear on which his mother had pinned the note saying she was leaving but that she would come get him real soon, right away, and that she loved him, and the Barbie doll his little sister had left behind even though it was the one she talked to more than to anything else. And other toys, many other toys he does not have now.

The boy knows it's a fantasy. All his reveries during which the hours with the accordion pass are empty. The only thing real is the squealing box in his hands and the sheet on the music stand from which he can not make out the melody. And the electric guitar in his head. Which can play all the melodies and knows all the ways.

The boy wonders: How did his father guess the electric guitar was so dangerous? How did he know not to get him one when he asked for it? How did he know it would spew fire if it came into the hands of the boy? His father told him that this accordion was the very same one he himself had played, and his father and grandfather before him, and that there'd be no guitar in his house. He meant in his room, because they live in a room, not a house, but the boy understood anyway. And marveled. True, his father knows about music, he's forever bringing him new sheets of music and placing them on top of the ones the boy has looked at to exhaustion. But how could he also know the secret of the electric guitar, which is hidden to all and has only been revealed to the boy? Every time the boy told his friends how the electric guitar could bring back the dead and shake up the living so that not a trace of life remained in their bodies, they'd giggle and wink at one another, and then when he fell silent and turned away they whispered behind his back that he was a bit touched. Yes, he heard it quite distinctly: A bit touched. But he was never touched by anyone or anything except when his father touched him too hard, far too hard. He knew what the phrase meant: They thought he was a bit off. That there was something wrong with him. He clenched his fists and kept silent. And thought to himself: If I had an electric guitar I'd show them. They think an electric guitar's just a thing those who know how can make produce sounds. And that these sounds are no more than that: Just sounds. What do they know! They don't know that the electric guitar has a will of its own, a life of its own, and that you have to be careful around it. Very careful.

The boy glances at the accordion in his hands, the cold, dead object which wheezes shapeless noises. He feels like flinging it on the ground and jumping up and down on it. Possibly, just possibly that might give it some pep. But no matter what, it would never become an electric guitar. Just as he – the boy knows – will never become that boy in the white tuxedo with the bow tie, on the concert hall stage, holding a violin in his hand and bowing while the audience claps effusively. And just as his father's belt will never become his mother's tarragon cake which she used to bake every Sunday when his father still let her out of the house to buy the groceries.

Over and over the boy grapples with the same shaky tune. He can't do it, he just can't do it. The keys evade him and the boy knows he won't make it. Somewhere in the corner, in the corner of the room, in the corner of his head, in the corner of the universe, there lurks the electric guitar.

Electricity gives power to all things, it's no wonder the boy can't manage without it. There's no music any more without electric power. It's no wonder his tunes are all squashed up and his fingers stumble over each other. I need an electric guitar, thinks the boy. Or at least electricity. It gives power to things.

Worriedly, the boy listens for sounds from the stairwell. For the time being he can't hear his father's heavy footfalls, but they will come before long. The boy knows that his father is seething with a rage he can barely control, and has been for a long time. The boy feels bad about it because he knows that his father loves him, and he has some idea how disappointed his father must be when he listens time and again to the boy hopelessly chasing after the melody. The boy remembers how often his father used to take him with him when he left home, and how they'd walk along the streets for hours on end and do nothing else, and how good it felt when his father put his arm around his shoulders. Except that one day when they came home his mother and his little sister were gone, and only the teddy bear and the Barbie doll remained. And the note that Mommy would come get him real soon. But she didn't. Not then and not later, though he waited.

His father explained to him that his mother and sister had left because women had no sense of duty, and that now they'd have to cope on their own, but the boy nevertheless felt that they could have stayed on where they were and needn't have moved to another town, where his father enrolled him in a different school and where they had a different name on the door and his father called him a different name which he didn't like half as much as the one before, though he'd already forgotten what that was. Where they used to live before, the apartment was bigger and the people were nicer. They'd often ask about his mother, about where she was, and they'd send their regards. Now there were no regards and nobody so much as knew that he'd ever even had a mother.

It occurs to the boy that the melody is unable to find its way out of the accordion. No, it won't work without power. He'll have to help the tune, it can't feel well, trapped in the choking bellows, it must want out, thinks the boy. Yes, electricity; the tune can't get out without power.

The boy finds the extension cord in the cupboard where his father keeps his tools. He turns over the accordion in his hands for a long time, unable to find an appropriate socket. First he blames it on the darkness, but finally it dawns on him that he's gone about it all wrong: It's the cord that needs to be changed to match the accordion, not the other way around. Using the knife he keeps under the pillow in case the dark man returns who used to bend over him at night and breathe hot air on him until he screamed and screamed and screamed, he cuts the cord on the end which doesn't plug into the wall, and strips apart every separate wire. Then, by touch alone, he attaches the individual wires to the frame of the accordion, until he feels they are all connected to something and that his work is done.

As he pushes the plug into the wall outlet, he hears a noise on the stairs. It's his father returning. He'll stumble on every step, then he'll be ever so long inserting the key in the lock, and the key will, as always, get stuck; then he'll get the door unlocked somehow, open it, and enter. The boy knows what lies in store for him, and it paralyzes him; he forgets about the accordion, about the sheet music spread out on the stand, about the instant soup he was supposed to be stirring into boiling water this moment because his father wants to eat when he comes home.

He squeezes into the gap between the wall and the closet, where he usually keeps his accordion, and hopes it will just go away, as it sometimes does, he hopes his father won't find the strength to listen to him play, that he'll just stagger over to bed and fall asleep without even kicking his shoes off. Then all the boy will have to do is cautiously remove them for him.

His father enters the room. He mutters indistinctly into his chin. He walks into the table, kicks over a chair with a crash. The boy presses further into the cranny, such a narrow space that his father, so he hopes, won't be able to follow. Because if he does follow, then, the boy knows, it's going to be bad, then it will be unending.

Although the room is filled with darkness, the father spots the accordion on the ground. He grumbles something sharply and bends over to pick it up, but as he takes hold of it he shudders, starts shaking, throws his head back, does a little offbeat dance of an unusual rhythm, and this goes on and on. Then the accordion slips from his fingers, and when it hits the ground the bellows emit a muffled moan, while the father collapses on the floor. He drools.

The boy waits. It's an ugly sight, gross, but he's seen it before. The boy reasons that his father didn't make it to bed this time. That's happened before too; he doesn't always make it. And so he doesn't need to take his shoes off either since there's no bed linen to get dirty.

The father does not move for a long time. The boy contemplates his next step. Usually, his father groans after a while, murmurs, yells. But nothing this time. Nothing. He lies motionless, still. The boy begins to realize it's different this time. And he doesn't know what to do.

At last he creeps out of his hiding place, unplugs the cord and puts it away, back into the cupboard. His father is always telling him to put things away; if you don't, you get covered with grime and dust, you need to put things away, be neat and tidy, scrub the dirt and dust off your body. And he scrubs the dust off the boy's body for a long, long time until the boy shivers under the spray of cold water since all the warm water has long been used up, and then his father picks him up and carries him to bed and draws his hand over his eyelids so that they close and then the boy can feel his father looking at him for a long, long time, and the boy knows that his father wishes him a good night and sweet dreams, and no dark man or hot breath on his cheek.

The boy looks at his father for a long, long time, but still the father does not budge. The boy thinks. He can't stay like this forever, he thinks. Finally he takes the keys out of his father's breast pocket. Although it sometimes takes his father a long time to locate the lock, he is always quick to put the keys carefully away. Always. The boy had already tried to open the door when he was home alone, to open the door and go to Africa to get the guitar, but he never once could find the keys. And the windows were so high up he got dizzy when he looked through them, there was a bottomless abyss beneath them.

The boy stands on the staircase and hesitates. His heart sinks because it is very dark already, and even if it were daylight, he does not know the way. There's not a single way he knows, because his father always accompanies him whenever he needs to go out, to go to school. But the boy knows he has no choice. There's only one option: He must find his mother. He'll ask on the corner if somebody knows her. He remembers her name, he's repeated it to himself over and over since she left, leaving behind that note. Somebody's bound to know her. If not on this corner, then on the next one or on the one after that; there is always at least one more corner. Sooner or later he'll find her. He knows: He must. He must find his mother. She'll know what to do next, she'll explain what happened. And maybe, just maybe she'll let him talk her into buying him an electric guitar.

Translated by Tamara Soban

Igor Bratož

Igor Bratož *was born in 1960. He studied at the Faculty of Arts in Ljubljana (major: Comparative Literature, minor: Sociology of Culture). He has published a collection of short stories The Gilding of Oblivion (Pozlata pozabe, 1988; Golden Bird Award) and was the co-author of the collection of stories Rošlin in Verjanko (1987). His short stories have been published in Austria, U. K., Hungary, U. S. A., Germany, Croatia, Greece and Czech Republic. He has translated into Slovene a number of American and English authors, among them Raymond Chandler, Richard Brautigan, Raymond Carver, Donald Barthelme, Woody Allen, Salman Rushdie and Harold Bloom. Since the summer of 2005 he is executive editor of the Literary supplement of Delo (largest Slovenian daily). He lives in Ljubljana with his wife and daughter.*

IMITATIO MUNDI
A Record of Triviality

Igor Bratož

> *All day I hear noise of waters*
> *Making moan,*
> *Sad as the sea-bird, when going*
> *Forth alone,*
> *He hears the winds cry to the waters*
> *Monotone.*

> James Augustine Aloysius Joyce
> Chamber Music XXXV

The sounds of Mozart's Requiem echoed in the high arched study. A bearded man in a black jumpsuit nodded his head and closed a textbook, the cover of which glittered with stylized microelectronic bands. Apparently satisfied with the information he had read there, he placed the book among the others in the crowded book shelf that covered the wall behind him and got up from his leather armchair. He pulled a tool that looked a screwdriver from a plastic bag and began fiddling with a large and complicated contraption equipped with a pilot's seat that

33

stood on a wooden stage at the centre of the strongly lit space. As he tested individual components in the massive frame that resembled a large black spider interwoven with countless wires, the long extended E of the recorded choir singing the Kyrie Eleison accompanied him.

He finished his work as the Mass ended. With a smile on his face, he put aside the electronic gauge and solemnly spoke into the sudden silence: "Each tone has its own meaning, like words, only they cannot be translated. Therefore: Back! To the roots of the source! Euterpa, stand by me now and for ever more!"

He placed two oblong black carrying cases on the back part of the contraption, sat down on the cushioned pilot's seat, put on his safety belt while pressing several different coloured buttons on the dashboard in front of him, and disappeared into the blinding light in which the study was suddenly submerged. In the next instant, he found himself on a stony bank of the Seine, Paris, August 1778.

Two very differently dressed men sat in the salon of a poorly maintained townhouse and sipped their afternoon tea. The bearded man in the black jumpsuit looked around with great curiosity. In addition to a round table, half covered with a faded crocheted cloth, and two unupholstered chairs and an empty birdcage, the only remaining piece of furniture was a neglected harpsichord. A pile of large format music paper scribbled with notes lay on top of its scratched surface. The other man, wearing a wig that had not seen powder for many days, stared motionless at the unusually dressed newcomer.

"And what, if I may be allowed ask, is your esteemed name, sir?" Wolfgang Amadeus Mozart asked inquisitively, pouring his guest and himself a fresh cup of tea. "Regrettably, there is no one here to properly introduce us," he added.

"I am what I am – but you may call me Viaggiatore," said Traveller.

34

"And what, may I be so bold, are you here for, Signor Viaggiatore?" Mozart was still curious.

"Everything and nothing, dear Mozart. I would like to talk about your music. Time," said Traveller, "is a funny thing, you know. Some who are now lost in time have called time gravedigger of all things and for a long time it was not clear if the remark was meant positively." Mozart still stared motionless at the newcomer. It seemed that he was not actually seeing him, but rather that he was staring into some measureless depths. Several times during Traveller's speech, he grabbed the edge of the tablecloth, twisted it hard and pulled it up under his nose with an absent air. "Where I come from," continued Traveller, "the future no longer interests us too much. Because we are able to imagine it in so many different ways, we know that it is as illusory as the autumn wind. And the present is mere fragments. What truly interests us are the great stories of the past; these are the strands that we weave into the great net where our own little stories are displayed." Traveller grew silent for a moment, then he quietly continued: "We are unique, I am unique, Mozart. That is why I am so interested in your music, in your work..."

"It is true, Signor Viaggiatore," Mozart responded with a weary voice, "that we never know for what heaven we work, or for what hell."

"Well, maestro, tell me, how are you doing? Your first performance in Paris was an extraordinary success. Some, however, claimed that you are Mozart no longer, that you are writing for Parisian taste, for local listeners."

"Paris is a devil," Mozart responded. "It's too far to walk anywhere or too muddy, and Paris, mysterious Signor, is indescribably dirty. If I go with a carriage, I need four to five liveried servants for the day – and for what?! – since people

35

here give praise but nothing else. If I am engaged for a certain day," Mozart exploded, "I play – and then I hear: *Oh, c'est un Prodige!* – and then farewell. When I first came, I invested a good deal of money in going around, though usually in vain, because I didn't even find people at home. If you don't live here, Signor Viaggatore, it is difficult to imagine how important that is. Paris has greatly changed and for some time now the French have not been as polite as they were fifteen years ago. Their behaviour is quite vulgar and they are unspeakably arrogant."

"And otherwise," the visitor asked, "how is it with work, money?"

"What can I say? Bad!" Mozart responded and fished out with his fingers a piece of cake that had dropped into his cup. "They make terrible mistakes when they print my music. I was offered the position of organist in Versailles, but I declined because I thought I might be able to find something better… and then nothing presented itself. It's not that I'm unwanted, it's just that Paris doesn't seem to need me. So there's no money. That damned Indian Dutchman," he scolded, gulping the tea-soaked cake down, "Dejeux[1] or I-don't-know-his-name-is paid me only a lice-ridden sixty-six sovereigns rather

---

[1] Mozart is speaking of the otherwise obscure Monsieur De Jean or Duchamp, an extraordinarily rich Dutch patron of the musical arts. Word had spread that he was also an excellent flautist. The composer no doubt made his acquaintance in Mannheim at the home of a flautist named Wendling. We know from Mozart's letter to his father dated December 10, 1777 that he received from Duchamp a commission for three concertinas and three short quartets for which he would receive two-hundred gold sovereigns. Because– and this with great delay – he only delivered a portion of the commissioned works, Duchamp was prepared to pay him less than the original amount. The term "Indian Dutchman" which we find in Mozart's letter probably refers to the fact that Duchamp made his money as the owner of an East Indian plantation.

36

than the promised two-hundred. Father didn't like him at all. And elsewhere it's no different. I gave the Duke of Guinness' daughter twenty-four two hour composition lessons and he tried to fob me off with three Louis d'or's which I declined."

"The flute quartets you mentioned before? I can tell you that they are first-rate, peerless," Signor Viaggiatore politely remarked.

"What are you saying to me..." Mozart shook his head and put down the empty teacup on the table.

"It is true, Mozart, it is true. Everyone agrees they are pearls..." Traveller reassured him. "They offer a flautist with extraordinary possibilities to show his virtuosity and display the tonal beauty of the instrument. In the opinion of many musicologists, they are a genuine party, a true divertimento."

"My word! But I can make no one understand me that I cannot bear the flute as a solo instrument in chamber music. It is as if everyone around here, especially the presumptuous philanthropists that crowd each evening around the Opéra-Comique, only want to hear the irritating overlapping of the violins and flutes, the empty embellishments, the same variations of the same musical arc... It seems to me that, more than the music, they are interested in those wanton girls who ought to be dispatched to Saint Lazare without delay," Mozart pungently concluded.

"There are other publics, maestro,"said Signor Viaggiatore, "perhaps not in Paris... but still..."

"Yes, but how are these other publics? And where are they? Who?" the incensed Mozart snorted, waving his hands.

"Expert audiences, shall we say. Specialists, if you like. In the fullness of time, there will be a deluge of words, too many words perhaps. Wendling, for example, the infallible arbiter of all things musical, analysed your D-Minor concert for piano and orchestra with such precision that he found a section for the piano that could only be properly played by a hand, if I am not mistaken, that is up in German lands, often unkindly called an Andalusian"[2]

The Traveller looked at the clearly annoyed Mozart and added in a conciliatory manner: "Well, given the speed with which you composed, mistakes would be understandable... excusable... by all means excusable..."

Mozart gave a dismissive wave of his hand and responded: "What could I do? It was the consequence of my ceaseless travelling. From Wasserburg across Augsburg, Hohen-Altheim, Mannheim, Metz and Clermont to Paris – it's a long, a very long and most tiring journey, Signor Viaggiatore. And that's not even mentioning the winter journey from Mannheim to Kirchheimbolanden to the court of Princess Caroline Nassau-Weilburg which was hardly cause for merriment."[3]

---

[2] There is an interesting section in the first movement of the concert. In two measures for the piano, Mozart wrote four low notes for the left hand (that are echoed by the strokes of the kettledrum) together with a chord two octaves higher – while at the same time, the right hand must play a quick arpeggio. Because it is obvious that the hand does not exist that could stretch three octaves, there are two theories that offer somewhat unusual, even bizarre explanations. More practical minds advocate the idea that the concert was written for an unusual kind of piano equipped with an additional pedal keyboard (as is known from the organ) with which the continuo could be executed. Today, the most explanation seems to be the following: that Mozart first wrote the bass notes and then changed his mind (we are talking about Mozart the genius!) only later adding the chord and forgetting to erase or at least cross out what he had written before. What the disputed part of the movement proves (if it proves anything at all) is that the travelling Mozart could not always be commended for his sobriety and composure when he sat down at the keyboard to compose in the morning.

[3] I. Barna somewhere wrote the following words: (...) in fact (he) did not compose anything much at all in the beginning of 1778. Instead, he plunged into social life, which earned him a rebuke in a letter from his father Leopold.

"Since we're talking about quartets," the curious Traveller continued the conversation, "would you mind telling me, please, when exactly did you write the A-major quartet?"[4]

"But how did you know? I'm tormenting myself with it right now. Commissions, as you know, must be delivered. It's going so badly that I would break the damned flute in two," Mozart said in a bad temper.

"Well, well, a little patience, maestro, not so angry. I know you will write it... I can hear it already." The mysterious Signor Viaggiatore sought to comfort Mozart with his quiet laughter. "Although," he continued with a more serious voice, "you do not yet know this and indeed I am probably the only

---

[4] Traveller is no doubt inquiring about Köchel-Verzeichnis 298, quartet number No. 4 in A-major for flute and strings. The original manuscript of the quartet has been preserved, though regrettably it is undated. Dr. Marie Oliver Georges Poulain Saint-Foix (1874-1945), a well-known researcher of the Mozart opus, concluded – on the basis of the fact that the last movement of the quartet is actually a series of variations on a theme from Paiseille's opera La Gare Generose (first performed in September 1786 in Vienna!) – that Mozart could only have composed the quartet after that year. However, another important researcher, Dr. Alfred Einstein (1880-1952), who reworked and reordered the list of Mozart's work previously compiled by Dr. Ludwig Ritter von Köchel, does not support this at first glance reasonable and well-argued assumption. He lucidly argues that, despite its astonishing melodic similarity to Paisielle's opera from 1778, the A-major quartet – the entire composition but especially the third move-ment – could be a light parody of the Quatours d'airs dialogues written by Giovanni Giuseppe Cambini (1746-1825), an otherwise minor Italian com-poser who resided in Paris but whose work was important for the develop-ment of Italian chamber music (sonatas) from the chivalrous period on-ward. Whatever the case may be, both theories could be faulted for a distressing lack of imagination since neither considers the possibility that Mozart might have been informed by someone – for instance, one of the mysterious black-clad strangers that in those days (as well as today) roamed through history – and thus was able to complete it eight years earlier.

person in these parts that does: the Österreichische Natio-
nalbibliothek in Vienna will acquire a manuscript of the quartet and on the margin the following words will be written
though not in your hand:

QUATOUR ORIGINAL COMPOSÉ PAR
WOLFGANG AMADEUS MOZART.
Á PARIS, 1778, MANUSCRIT DU
COMPOSITEUR, REÇU DU BARON
DE JACQUIN

Is what is written true? Do you confirm it?"

"But of course! The year is the right one… and the Baron,
the Baron is also my friend," responded the confused Mozart
and stood up with his arms crossed over his chest. "But,
Signor, let us put this aside, it is not even finished yet, it's not
even half way done… I'd rather you tell me something else…"

"Excellent," Traveller noisily interrupted him, and pulled a
notepad from the inside pocket of his jumper. "This information has inestimable value for music history. We are doing very
well. Please sit down."

"…but are you… possibly O.B.?[5]

That you know so much about myself and my work?" asked
Mozart, even more confused than before.

Traveller smiled fawningly. "No, no, not at all. I am your
faithful admirer, dear maestro, yes an admirer, and above all a
listener," he concluded and sat down once again. "My time,
you know, is a time of listening, of eavesdropping on lost
fragments," he added more seriously.

"And your opportunities are… how shall I say… limitless?
Virtually limitless?" It began to dawn on the composer.

---

[5] O.B. = Ordens-Bruder = monk, and specifically a brother (or member)
of the Freemasons Lodge.

"From your standpoint, and ... ha-ha, for that matter from mine... you could say that," mocked the Traveller, getting up and pacing the bleak room. "Would you like to listen to some music, Mozart? Perhaps it would calm you down. You seem a bit agitated."

"Yes, of course! Though you didn't answer my question. What music... are you thinking of? Where are the musicians?" Mozart asked dumbfounded. He sat down again.

Traveller lifted his palms in a gesture soliciting patience. "A moment, maestro," he said and pulled a small cassette player out of his pocket. "This is the orchestra! It's true that the machine has only twice twenty watts but the sound is as pure as tears! Pioneer! Made in Japan. Three heads, two motors... But why am I telling you this? Certainly you have no interest in such details."

"Right here? Inside?" Mozart looked closely at the shiny little box and shook his head in disbelief.

"Of course and why not?" Traveller answered easily. "Only a moment, maestro... hmm, what have we here?" Traveller rummaged through the contents of the black bag that he had taken with him on his voyage and at last pulled out a cassette. "How about something Italian to start with?" he murmured, putting the tape in the machine and pressing a button.

The pleasant sound of chamber music resounded through the salon. For some time, the two men listened in silence.

"Why that, that is quite exceptional," Mozart sighed after a while, "the music as well. Whose is it?"

"Paisiello. From the opera *La Gare Generoso*. The overture," Signor Viaggiatore answered. "Vienna will praise him to the skies for it in a couple of weeks and then will forget all about it just as they will forget the gleaming finery of ladies of Schönnbrun Palace. Aha... he will write that in 1786."

"It's quite good..." Mozart stammered, "or rather it will be quite good. Although I think it could be done differently...

41

indeed, I think I'll use a little section for my quartet. Play some more, please, I would listen again. I am beginning to believe in fragments myself. I can't quite explain the feeling to you... a sort of emptiness that hurts me... a kind of longing that will never be satisfied. It never stops... it continues forever... growing from day to day... the unusual feeling that you are building from fragments and yet a few are always missing... yes, yes, please, play some more ..."

Traveller smiled to hear the composer's words. "Why, you speak like someone from my era, maestro. As if you knew... but it's just talk about the creative process. Where the heart is, this they don't talk about. The heart beats its rhythm of opening and closing books and the tears flow through the galleries. Yes, in fact they live from the labyrinths of their libraries, music collections, discographies."

Traveller changed the cassette and a solo voice singing German lieder sounded in the salon. The two men quietly listened until the end.

"There is nothing I enjoy about being alone when something is bothering me, but now please, I beg you to leave me alone," Mozart said, standing up. "I must work... my patrons are waiting for each and every note. Please call again tomorrow. At any hour."

"At your service," Traveller responded and left.

After only a few minutes a loud rapping was heard at the door and Signor Viaggatore stood at the threshold with an even larger black carrying case in his hand. "I'd almost forgotten – a gift for you." He carefully placed the oblong case on the cover of the harpsichord and opened it. A keyboard shimmered from the cushioned interior.

"This, maestro, is the most recent technological achievement from the Far East... It includes a computer... and a printer... how can I explain? It is the mechanism that makes the keyboard and the computer function at all. But if you wait another ten years, I believe a certain Luigi Galvani will invent...frog's croaking... milk... lettuce... Oh, it's a long story ... one of the many ...."

"Excuse the question, sir, but you will understand: my pen is quite old and my instruments as well. I have been shitting from the same hole for the last twenty-two years and it has not torn... And how many times I have shat... in one way or another. Understand me, the victory over doubts must be deliberate. So, I ask you, how do I even use this portable harpsichord?" Mozart asked, gently stroking the keyboard with his fingers.

"Any way you like, Mozart!" Traveller answered. "Little yellow-skinned people have made it in such a way that you can compose on it in nine-hundred and ninety-nine ways and that is not even counting its use as an instrument of torture. You may select any sound or murmur that you like and would care to use in your composition: for example, the murmuring of waves thirty-three ways, the howling of the wind, the tone of the organ, the harpsichord, horns, harps, flutes, whistles, violas, violins, two violins, the noble chords of a hundred violins... Once you have written the composition, you can repeat it, correct it, modulate it, try different combinations of instruments, add percussions, even the echo of the concert hall, and thousands of other effects. By simply pressing down a button, the notes of the whole composition will be automatically printed on note paper – the possibilities are infinite... Or as the most recent propaganda of the truly fanatical put it: with this keyboard, Ludwig could have composed twice what he did in a third of the time..." Viaggatore finished his speech using the tones of an advertising executive.

"I'm utterly enchanted," Mozart cried. "I shall keep it!"

"I wish you great enjoyment and inspiration, maestro," said the visitor in black as he departed, wondering if it was a gift or a betrayal.

43

The gas lanterns burned in the house of Wolfgang Amadeus as he sat awestruck and touched the keyboard that lay casually on the harpsichord in the centre of the salon as if on a stage of sorts. He began run his fingers playfully over the beautiful and surprisingly uniform keys, all the while staring out the window into the depth of the Parisian night. A number of different melodies could be heard in the night, now something inquisitive and warm similar to an Italian divertimento, now something filled with yearning like a Hoffmeister pastoral, then a weightless French amusement...[6]

Mozart played with increasing vivacity and excitement throughout the night. All of a sudden, he stood up in the middle of a cadence. He stared as if struck at the glimmering light through the window. "Of course," he cried out, "that is the only possible way," and he excitedly began to pound on the keyboard. On the computer screen, the green glowing word at the beginning of the last measure RONDEAU disappeared and was replaced by RONDIEAOUS. In place of the usual tempo for the rondo, allegro or allegretto, Mozart eagerly typed out the following words.

Allegretto grazioso, ma non
troppo, presto, però non troppo
adagio, cosi-cosi, con molto
garbo ed espressione.

"In, aha … this also," he exhaled, leaning over keyboard. On the screen at the end of the notes, the following symbols appeared:

---

[6] It seems redundant to remark that music historians most often cite the aforementioned Paisielle's opera as the source of the A-major quartet, followed by the song *An die Natur* by Franz Anton Hoffmeister and of course the the old French rondeau *Il a des bottes, des bottes Bastein.*

D. S. AL. S. SENZA FINE

– dal segno al segno senza fine which would become the prevailing notation of the composition into infinity… a musical loop, the musical imitation of all that is imitable.

Morning.

"And how did it go, Wolferl of Salzburg?" Signor Viaggiatore asked ceremoniously.

"Perhaps you wondered or even believed that I had died? – perished? – kicked the bucket?" Mozart exclaimed. "But no, I beg of you, never think such a thing, because to think and to shit one's pants are two very different activities. How could I write something so beautiful if I were dead? How could it be possible? Back! – from the roots to the source…"

He pressed a button and took from the keyboard's printer a sheet of music for the quartet and, with an unfathomably mysterious smile, handed it to his visitor in black. Traveller took one glance at the paper and immediately penetrated the meaning of the pernicious musical loop. As if struck mad, he ran from the house and threw the paper into the Seine.

The river carried the paper toward the sea and from that time on, say those instructed in such matters, the ebb and flow of the tides alternate in an orderly rhythm. Some more musically sensitive souls seem to hear above the splashing of the waves the sound of distant instruments, heavenly echoes, glorious music. Oceanographers do rule this out.

Evening.

"And how did it go, Wolferl of Salzburg?" Signor Viaggiatore asked ceremoniously.

"Perhaps you wondered or even believed that I had died? – perished? – kicked the bucket?" Mozart exclaimed. "But no, I beg of you, never think such a thing, because to think and to shit one's pants are two very different activities. How could I write something so beautiful if I were dead? How could it be possible? Back! – from the roots to the source..."

He pressed a button and took from the keyboard's printer a sheet of music for the quartet and, with an unfathomably mysterious smile, handed it to his visitor in black. Traveller took one glance at the paper and immediately penetrated the meaning of the pernicious musical loop. As if struck mad, he ran to the window, hurriedly opened it, and threw the paper into the dark courtyard.

The wind lifted the paper. Somewhere above the ground, a black bird seized the rustling sheet and flew off into the night. From that day on, say those instructed in such matters, the morning warbling of the birds became harmonious. Some more musically sensitive souls seem to hear in the parks and the woods the sound of distant instruments, heavenly echoes, glorious music. Ornithologists do not rule this out. [7]

Morning.

"And how did it go, Wolferl of Salzburg?" Signor Viaggiatore asked ceremoniously.

"Perhaps you wondered or even believed that I had died? – perished? – kicked the bucket?" Mozart exclaimed. "But no, I beg of you, never think such a thing, because to think and to

---

[7] According to Wolfgang Hildesheimer, Mozart always liked to keep some sort of bird with him. First he had a starling. That was followed by a canary that the composer, a few days before his death, had removed from his room. In any case, the starling was very important in his life. On May 27, 1784, he bought it for thirty-four Austrian kreutzers, including the cage, and the two lived together for the following three years. If we are to believe Mozart's own records – and there is no reason why we wouldn't – the starling knew how to sing the first five measures from the rondo of the piano concert in G major (Köchel-Verzeichnis 453). Existing scholarship, as we have indicated, does not rule this out.

shit one's pants are two very different activities. How could I write something so beautiful if I were dead? How could it be possible? Back! – from the roots to the source..."

He pressed a button and took from the keyboard's printer a sheet of music for the quartet and, with an unfathomably mysterious smile, handed it to his visitor in black. Traveller took one glance at the paper and immediately penetrated the meaning of the pernicious musical loop. As if struck mad, he ran to the fireplace and through the paper into the flames.

A small cloud of white smoke rose from the chimney into the evening sky and from that day on, say those instructed in such matters, the order of the stars in the night sky has been calmly balanced. Some more musically sensitive souls seem to hear in the signs of the stars the sound of distant instruments, heavenly echoes, glorious music. Astrologists do not rule this out.

Morning.

"And how did it go, Wolferl of Salzburg?" Signor Viaggiatore asked ceremoniously.

"Perhaps you wondered or even believed that I had died? – perished? – kicked the bucket?" Mozart exclaimed. "But no, I beg of you, never think such a thing, because to think and to shit one's pants are two very different activities. How could I write something so beautiful if I were dead? How could it be possible? Back! – from the roots to the source..."

He pressed on a button and took from the keyboard's printer a sheet of music for the quartet and, with an unfathomably mysterious smile, began to play his composition. Those instructed in such matters say that he is still playing it somewhere. Those more musically sensitive seem to hear, on quiet evenings or when they reflect on the depths of time, the sound of distant instruments, heavenly echoes, glorious music. Psychiatrists do not rule this out.

Translated by Erica Johnson Debeljak

Aleš Čar

Aleš Čar *was born in 1971 in Idrija, a mining town in western Slovenia. He studied comparative literature at the Faculty of Arts and Sciences in Ljubljana. A writer, publicist, translator and scriptwriter, he has published two novels, Igra angelov in netopirjev (A Play of Bats and Angels, 1977) and Pasji tango (Dog Tango, 1999), as well as a collection of short stories V okvari (Out of Order, 2001).*

THE FLOORS

Aleš Čar

I've seen torture that shines like stars. I know that almost everyone feels at least something about it but, except for me, I don't know anyone who's really seen it. When one person dominates another person to the point that the first begins to collapse either mentally or physically, then both are liberated. And energy. Enormous energy.

For me, torture has always been an act of love. It is my gift to enjoy humiliation that verges on total collapse. I enjoy it at least as much as whoever's up on top in a state of pleasure, domination and splendor. Destruction is giving and taking at the same time. To know how to exist at the opposite extreme is giving and taking squared. No, it's not a religion. Erase that shit. It's just my world.

I grew up in a normal, proper, happy family in Trieste. My father ran a men's clothing boutique. My parents and my brother still live in Trieste. My brother runs the boutique now. He's five years older than me, serious, reserved, loyal and dedicated.

Because of both his physical beauty and his mental limitations, he's always been my polar opposite. It's no wonder that right from the beginning I felt like he was more than just a big brother to me, and I more than just his sister. My masochism and humiliation have always meant the destruction of everything that was unattainable to me from birth.

As long as I can remember, I've had a special attitude toward pain. First physical pain. When I was little, I used to pinch the flesh on the inside of my thigh because it calmed me down. I pinched and kneaded the skin so much that it turned black. One summer afternoon, my brother was fixing his bike in the little garage next to the boutique and I was sitting on the ground watching the birds in the street. My brother went somewhere and left me holding the pliers in my hand. I squeezed until the skin and the top layer of flesh began to tear away from my thigh. That was the first time I drew blood. When I stopped, excited and sweaty, full of strange energy, there was a mutilated piece of flesh – black and numb. Insensitive to pain.

Then I took a stapler, needles and sewing scissors from my father's store and a hammer and pliers from my brother's workshop. I held the stapler and slowly pressed it down on my skin. I was surprised by the ease with which it slid through the skin and how fresh, exciting and different was this specific feeling of pain. How different it was from what I would feel if I fell from a bicycle for example. With this pain, there was a certain feeling of satisfaction as if I was hurting something that had no connection to me. I ran a needle into my skin perpendicular to the staple. Then I went to the bathroom for iodine, gauze and a bandage, returned to the room, looked at it, took my father's scissors and, beneath the cross made by the needle and the staple, cut out a small piece of my thigh. The pain shook me, it was terrible, but feelings of fulfillment, excitement and warmth followed. I disinfected and wrapped the wound, I put away the tools in the dresser drawer and then I put the piece of flesh into my mouth and chewed. It hurt, of course, but the warmth and the excitement grew stronger. I had never felt anything like it before.

Nothing had ever excited me to that degree. Perhaps it was then that I experienced my first orgasm. The whole procedure lasted about an hour and a half. When I regained awareness, the piece of my thigh was no longer in my mouth.

Of course, I did all of this in an unconscious sort of way. I wasn't thinking about anything. I was only aware of the warmth of my aroused body, which I later cooled down against a cool wall. It is hard for me to describe to you how I felt at that moment. My body, which up until then had always been an obstacle for me, somehow opened inward. I was utterly ravished. I was shocked.

Now I feel enthusiastic about my former naiveté. Then I thought I had discovered something that others would also want if they only dared to try it. Something dark and forbidden, like sex. Of course, I didn't understand why it was forbidden. Actually, I still don't know who is the victim, the evil that is on top of me when I voluntarily give my body over to punishment, or me.

I brought Mateja, my brother's wife, to the house for the first time. I had spotted her at the birthday party of a boy in the neighborhood. I usually hid in a corner at those kind of events, longing for a kindred spirit. Mateja was new on the street and kept to herself. She was a pretty girl with blond hair tied up with a blue band, but her beauty wasn't classic like a Barbie doll. A narrow mouth and too small nose gave her a strange absent-minded look. It was her absence that caught my eye (and, I believe, her absence that my brother later fell in love with). I stepped toward her and she give me one strange look and we clicked. We talked all night and became friends. One week ago, I heard her voice after many years over the telephone. My brother had called because he'd seen my mutilated body on television. He asked me if I needed anything, if I was okay. Tell me if you need money, he said, tell me what you need. Then I heard Mateja's voice in the background. She was screaming that both Matic and I were sick, that they should lock me up or take me to the lunatic asylum because I was crazy. I knew that she was finally saying what she had had in her head since the age of 12, since the time we became friends.

Most of the time, we hung out in my room. I don't know what we did exactly. I have a picture in my head of her holding a teddy bear without arms, a doll without a head, and me working with a pair of pliers on a piece of wood from the edge of my bed. Once I took the teddy bear from her, tied a rope around his neck and hung him from a light fixture. She thought it was funny. A couple of days later, I tore the legs of the plastic doll off and stabbed her in the stomach with a pair of scissors. Mateja didn't say anything. Then I went too far. I carried the parrot in the cage from the living room to my room. First we just looked at it and talked to it, then we let it out of the cage and chased it around the room. When I finally caught it, I tied the rope around one leg and used the pliers to hold the other one. The pliers were just heavy enough so he could only fly up about five centimeters and then fall down, then up then down. We both laughed. I know now that she's the same as I am deep inside and that's why she hates me. I also know that she practices the same sort of thing on my brother, safely hidden behind four walls, dulled by some strong pills, just enough so it can still be called a normal marriage with a dominant wife. And I also know that, with what I have learned now, I could bring her to the point where her mind would grow foggy, where she would waver at the edge, not knowing where the pleasure was coming from or where she was falling to. But back then, I was young and rash. Things got out of hand. I grabbed the parrot and shoved a needle through its closed beak. The end of the needle came out the other side of its head. I remember the silence. The silence of the parrot that looked at

54

me in surprise, the warmth of the fog in my head. Mateja gaped open-mouthed, not knowing whether to believe her eyes. After a few seconds, she ran out of the room screaming and I opened the window and tossed the parrot on the roof of the neighbor's house. A little while later, the door opened and my mother walked in.

"Mateja's father telephoned," she said, "Mateja's completely beside herself. She said you put a needle through Piki's head."

"She's lying," I said. "He flew out the window. It's her fault. She opened it."

That night I cried because I knew I'd lost something big. I think I knew that from then on I'd be alone. I was only 13 years old but I'd already completely separated myself from normal eroticism and from the rest of the world. From sympathy, love, intimacy at little parties, which in any case was no problem because nobody ever invited me anywhere anyway, much less looked at me. I didn't really expect anything anymore. Actually by that time, I'd accepted my unbelievable physical ugliness as something special, as something that determined my life, something that sent me on my own solitary path.

A couple of months later, Mateja made friends with my brother and later they got married.

For a long time after that, nothing much happened. I needed time. Sometimes I climbed through the window at night, out to the balcony and down to the ground. I walked along the piers, hid in the shadows, watched the homeless drunks, the woman who lay on the ground with her head in the trash. I think my parents knew what I was doing but turned a blind eye. As they did with other things. When I came home, one would go to the bathroom and the other would stand outside my door. But that was all.

In the summer, a house on the neighboring street was left empty. Some bums immediately took over the second floor and the attic and I discovered a narrow hole that led into the basement. I crawled through it and found a black cat among the cartons, cupboards and other junk. Although animals had broken my heart many times as people never had, I began to regularly torture animals. I cleaned up the basement, swept, fixed the windowsills, used a shelf from one of the cupboards to prepare a surface where I arranged my tools. First I would caress the captured cat, comb its fur, pet it. Without trust, it's not exciting. I didn't know then what I was looking for. Now, of course, I know that trust and its expansion represents an important volume of the feeling that ultimately exploded when the animal, with a flash of self-consciousness, realized what was happening to it, became aware of its condition, the life that was slowly flowing from it, its death. The depth of shock was an important ingredient. When the nail suddenly penetrated its paw, the gradual confusion and the emptiness in its eyes when it understood what was to come – fear, hope, crawling, begging – then the second nail – flight and panic – then the third and fourth nail, an incision of the knife, the pressure of the pliers, the pulled out claws, emptied out eyes socket, the loss of consciousness and the horror at reviving in the same situation until finally I pulled the nails out, disinfected its wounds and let it run free. Today I know that the reason for my excitement was not my domination, but my identification with the cat. More important than the pain I gave was my empathy with the cat who suddenly found itself broken on the table with a ball of putty in its mouth, looking at me, its tormentor.

I thought about what I'd done and how I would continue. I killed only rarely. With death, my fulfillment was replaced by apathy. Instead of excitement, mere slaughter. One night I ripped open a cat's stomach, rinsed the internal organs in water, put them back in and stitched the cat up. I wouldn't be able to say why I did it, except perhaps that it had to do with research and, of course, that if you dare to set off on such a path, you get all kinds of ideas. After all, death was beautiful. It was something I was always approaching. With torture, I toyed with death because I could never be sure if my tormentor, in his pleasure, would know how to stop his power on the thin edge between the psychic and physical collapse of his victim. Death is beautiful as something distant, omnipresent and accidental, like the beauty of a crumpled corpse in a car crash that you pass on the way to work.

I tortured cats, bandaged their wounds and then – disfigured, limping, with only one eye or entirely blind, without claws or with a broken paw, without ears or a tail – returned them to the street. They were my little spirits populating the streets of Trieste. As they hobbled along the streets, people paused full of compassion, shaking their heads in horror. Others even kneeled down to the sidewalk and tried to pet them, but they panicked and took flight – as much as they were able. Trieste was soon full of mutilated cats, dogs, pigeons and sparrows. Rumors began to circulate. I remained hidden in the crippling shadows and swallowed my compassion for everything normal.

By the age of 16, I knew I needed a living person. I started by reading and researching my world. I didn't care about the gender of the person (so I suppose I'm bisexual). I needed only a clear structure of emotions, consciousness, self-consciousness, a complex of thoughts, desires and needs. And all of these feelings are precisely differentiated only in human beings.

The fundamental mechanism was clear to me. My special relationship to physical pain had crystallized in physical masochism balanced out by a strong desire for psychological sadism. For the perfect fulfillment of these two poles of pleasure, I needed, as I said, a real person. A human person.

When I was 18, I moved to Ljubljana to study. I did very well in school. The first and only exam I failed was in the second year with a professor of social anthropology. I must have been nervous, because I knew everything; I had studied with ease and pleasure. When I came the second time, I was the last name on the list to retake the oral exam. I entered the room already angry, but then the professor wrote the highest grade next to my name – no questions – and invited me out for coffee. That's how I got to know the most important woman in my life, a necrophiliac with a brilliant university career. She knew what she was doing. My intelligence and extreme physical shortcomings were a temptation for someone who experienced the erotic dimension of being and of love a little bit differently. I was enthusiastic, eager to comply. I undressed, put a needle between my teeth and lay limp on the floor like a cadaver. Usually she would put me in a bath filled with cold water and draw a corpse's mask on my face, sometimes bluish, sometimes all cut up. Then she pulled me on to the floor and performed cunnilingus on my cold dead labia in which she had inserted a piece of ice. With the needle, I repeatedly perforated my tongue and the roof of my mouth. When we were near orgasm, she came up close to my face and I let the blood pour from my mouth, as if from a corpse, and she smeared it on her breasts.

The other was a drug addict who worked at the pharmacy: a lesbian and a pretty unattractive woman (though nothing compared to me). Sometimes we got together and she always gave me a big dose of morphine analgesics against the pain that came after the fact when it was no longer welcome.

Then came Matic, my one and only true love in life. Now that he's dead, my scarred and mutilated body in the newspapers, on television and everywhere else, people ask me how I can speak of love. Like this: we met at the zoo in front of the monkey cage. I threw them a piece of bread with a needle pushed into the center. He saw what I had done and started to laugh. I asked him what was so funny but he didn't say anything, just looked at me and nodded. For a couple of minutes, I thought he was mute but then he spoke and I realized he had an unbelievable stutter. We went for a coffee and brandy and after every shot he became more relaxed and spoke more smoothly. That's how we found each other (it was the first time for both of us). An hour later, I knew he loved me.

He was studying to become a veterinarian. He had an excellent, that is to say photographic memory. By nature, he was shy and gentle. He was a subtle emotional creature. Too subtle. The only medicine for his hypersensitivity (and his stuttering) was drink. With each glass, he got better. In one particular phase of intoxication, he actually became funny. But alcohol made him worse in terms of analytical or synthetic thought. All together, it was the right combination for me: mental limitations, exceptional emotional sensitivity, impotence and excellent knowledge of the anatomy. He knew how to strike me and stab me without damaging any vital organs. He read my body like an instrument of pain. And he could take an unbelievable quantity of my verbal maltreatment and humiliating abuse.

Six months after we met, he asked me to marry him. I didn't know what to say. I told him that in time, that might mean something to me. I said that I would. After a couple of months, I moved in with him and because everything seemed normal, I stayed. We both graduated. Matic became a bureaucrat at the Ministry of Agriculture and I went on to work on my masters with my favorite professor. He didn't like that and I knew I had an extremely jealous person on my hands. At first, I was afraid of this; later it turned out to be a welcome mechanism for driving things to the very edge. Matic went to work, I wrote my thesis and worked around the house and weekends it was just the two of us (neither of us maintained any contact with our families). On Saturdays, we went on little trips and Sundays were the day for our games. He would start drinking beer in the morning, and I quickly lost my temper. At lunch, I would bang the table, turn over the plates and scream. In the afternoon, when his eyes became glassy, I attacked him with anything that came into my head. His limitations, his impractical nature, his asociability, his effeminate ways, his frustration, psychological suppression, childishness, impotence and his humiliatingly tiny penis which actually was the reason behind everything else. When we were at the edge of explosion I went to visit my professor, which drove him, jealous as he was, out of his mind. I would have a couple of drinks with her. When I came home, it was usually necessary to say only one more little thing to him in order to make him grab me by the hair, bang my head against the wall, go after me with his fists, throw me to the floor and kick me, pull me by my hair around the apartment, push my head into the toilet, throttle me in the bathtub, stab me in my thighs with needles, burn my stomach with cigarettes, send a stream of urine into my mouth and on my face, shove the tube of a turned-on vacuum cleaner in one of my three orifices.

It was the first time in my life that I loved someone. Really loved someone. Two years after I moved in with him, I finally decided that we should get married. A couple of weeks later we did and then everything went to hell.

I don't have any illusions. Matic destroyed any I had. I alone am guilty. That's not a complaint, that's a fact. Now I bang myself on the head. It was clear, logical, like everything was before, but now it's all over. He, of course, understood marriage in the most banal sense, in the most everyday sense. Clearly, he only understood what was there to understand. I should have seen that.

It started with his jealousy that became morbid. He wanted me to cut off all connection with the two women in my life. I simply couldn't do that because I was, among other things, finishing my thesis. And, in any case, I didn't have any desire to end my relationships with them, sexual or otherwise. The transformation occurred in a synchronous fashion: he began to drink more and more but instead of a culmination of violence he broke down. He began to tremble, to cry and to ask me if I loved him: "Do you really? Do you really love me?" When this happened the fourth or fifth time, I realized what it meant and what was happening. The man was falling apart before my eyes.

He started to come home drunk from his job. And he kept drinking. In the evening, he usually cried and asked me if I loved him. It became a real nightmare. I was home less and less, at my professor's house more. I rented a separate apartment for myself. Because of his drinking, he was fired from his job. Then he was home all day and just drinking. I got my degree in the fall and applied for a position as an assistant professor. I tried to talk to him; I wanted to convince him that he had to get better, that he urgently needed rehabilitation, that that was the only way to get a new start. Nothing. Six months after these barren struggles with a ruined man, I packed my bags and moved out. It was April. A month later the police found his body decaying in the living room. The neighbor had called because of the stench that spread from the apartment. He simply poisoned himself with drink. He was buried on the first day of January.

Two weeks later, two detectives came to my door. They told me they wanted to verify some information and ask me some questions. The neighbors in the apartment told them what happened between Matic and me. Especially on weekends. From arguments and screaming to breaking things up and violent fights. The police told me that, though only my screams had been heard, the neighbors said that it was hardly probable that Matic, a modest and gentle man, was capable of giving such a beating. They seemed to realize that Matic was incapable of squashing even a cockroach. They asked me if he had beaten me, or I him, and if I had any way of proving it. Even today I don't know why I did it. I could have convinced them in other ways; I'm sure of it. I took off by blouse and let my wide pants fall to the floor. They simply couldn't breathe. Scars, bruises, incisions. They looked at the floor and told me to get dressed. They didn't ask anything else. A little while later, activists from a women's help group knocked on my door. And after them, journalists. My story about abused women exploded in the media like a bomb. It shook the living and the dead. More journalists came, then the radio, then television. I became the torture victim, the symbol of persecuted women. An apostle for the suffering, the hungry, the sick. I became an advertise-ment on television, a picture on billboards around town. I became CocaCola.

Translated by Erica Johnson Debeljak

Evald Flisar

Evald Flisar is a novelist, short story writer, playwright, essayist, and editor of the oldest Slovenian literary journal Sodobnost, published since 1933. He studied comparative literature at the University of Ljubljana, Slovenia, and English in London, where he spent 17 years of his life, editing (among other things) an encyclopeadia of science and writing stories and radio plays for the BBC. From 1995 to 2002 he was president of the Slovene Writers' Association. His work has been translated into 25 languages (including Icelandic, Arabic, Malay, Bengali, Marathi and Hindi). He has traveled in more than 80 countries and held public readings worldwide, from Australia to the United States, from South America to Scandinavia. His best known novel is Going away with the wild tiger (Čarovnikov vajenec, first edition 1986, seventh edition 2007). Flisar has written fourteen plays, among them What about Leonardo (Best Play of the Year Award, produced in many countries, also in London's West End), Tomorrow (Prešeren Fund Award), produced in eighteen countries, and Nora Nora (Best Play of the Year Award), also produced in many countries. His Collected Plays were published in 2006 by Texture Press in New York. He has published two collections of short stories.

EXECUTIONERS

Evald Flisar

The next morning we cycled to Pathan, in better times known as Lalitpur, "the city of beauty". Six months into the journey, our hope of finding a place that would be "magic", "undefiled" and "different", was as clear as ever. But as we negotiated our way through littered alleways, trying to avoid chickens, dogs and piles of excrement, it began to dawn on us that our expectations were once again on a collision course with reality. Pathan was a provincial market town of open sewers and crumbling facades, its ancient beauty buried under the pungent layer of Himalayan squalor.

We dismounted near a cluster of food stalls on a tiny square. We looked around for a place to leave our borrowed bicycles, so we could go for a stroll. Their owner in Kathmandu had warned us not to forget that Nepalese people "not at all like to walk". As we stood there wondering what to do, a barefoot urchin detached himself from a group of children nearby. Hesitantly, he sauntered towards us. His runny nose was badly in need of a handkerchief. His round, discolored cap was tilted to one side, making him look like something of a rogue. As he came closer he greeted us with a courageous smile.

"Grrr, grrr," he said, quickly adding, "ga, ga, grrr, brrr, ek, ek, bhrrr." Seeing our puzzled faces, he took another step towards us and repeated, "Grrr, brrr, ek, bbbhhhrrrggrrr!"

Whatever language that was - and it sounded like a mixture of half a dozen – the boy was obviously trying to tell us something. He took hold of the handlebars and began to pull the bicycle away from me. He rushed to the wall of the nearby building and tapped it repeatedly with his fingers.

"Grrr, brrr, ek, grrr," he insisted.

Of course! The boy had seen our predicament and approached to offer advice. He was suggesting that we lean our bicycles against the wall, where, judging by the expression on his face, they would be perfectly safe. In the absence of any alternatives, we did just that. This encouraged him to offer more help. As I bent down to secure the bike with an old-fashioned chain, his face suddenly popped up between my legs.

"Grrr, grrr," he muttered and tugged at my trousers. He snatched the key from my hand and engaged in a brief struggle with the rusty lock. The job completed, he assaulted the lock on my wife's bicycle. That took a bit longer, but he was determined to finish what he had started.

"Grrr, brrr," he proclaimed, glowing with pride. As I reached for the keys, the boy shook his head and hid them behind his back. Then he rushed towards me and skillfully dropped them into my trouser pocket. Finally he stepped back and, looking from one to the other, waited for a sign of approval.

I smiled and tickled him under he chin. First there was an audible sigh of relief, then a gurgle of happy laughter, which was followed by half a dozen leaps in the air.

"What's your name?" I asked him when he calmed down.

He failed to respond; he was to busy showing us ff to his friends who had rushed over to see what was happening.

I repeated the question, but again there was no response. It was my wife who realised that the boy was deaf as well as dumb.

Moving my lips very slowly, I repeated, "What is your name?"

His eyes clouded over. Unable to understand me, he wouldn't be able to please me. He seemed terrified at the prospect. He turned to his chums, but they were at as much of a loss as he was.

One clever little girl suddenly understood. "Uki," she shouted, pointing at our snotty-nosed little friend, "Uki!"

The boy, greatly relieved, gurgled with laughter and added, "Grrr, grrr, ek, ek!" Grabbing hold of my hand, he began to pull me across the square. He had decided to show us the sights. Excitedly, he drew pictures in the air of pagodas, carvings, statues, or so it seemed. Jumping about in front of us like a rabbit, he led us down a side alley and round a corner into the main square. The square was surrounded by exquisite temples, finer and more elaborate than any we had seen in Nepal. The view was breathtaking. The "city of beauty" had come alive.

"Grrr, grrr, brrr, ek," the boy explained, suddenly sombre and self-important. This was his town, those were his temples, he owned all that beauty. And he was giving it all to us as a present.

We followed him round the square, from building to building, pausing to let him point out pillars and spires, and to draw our attention to particularly interesting carvings. "Grrr, grrr, brrr, ek, ek, brrr," he gurgled happily, basking in his role.

Afraid that we might get bored, he stole an occasional glance at our faces. Every time he noticed the slightest sign of growing disinterest, he slapped his forehead as if he had remembered that just round the corner there was another architectural wonder. To make him happy, we expressed appreciation of whatever he chose to point out, even if it was only a crumbling wall.

It soon became obvious that Uki's eagerness was not entirely selfless. He was hoping that at the end of the guided tour he would gain himself a rupee or two. Dressed as he was, in a thin short-sleeved shirt and a pair of bedraggled old trousers, he could certainly win the sympathy of even the stingiest foreigner.

We entered the courtyard of the royal bath-house, which was guarded by a solitary soldier. He and Uki were obviously friends.

"Grrr, brrrr," said the boy as we entered. He paused in front of the soldier, snapped to attention and saluted. The soldier, little more than a boy himself, gave him a friendly grin and saluted back. After a brief tour of the bath-house we decided to take a rest. We sat down on an exposed beam near the entrance. A little earlier my wife had bought some bananas, and now she offered one to Uki.

He wasn't quite sure what to do with it. He laughed, became serious, laughed again.

"Grrr, brrr, brrr," he explained finally and pushed the banana behind the string that held up his trousers. With an pologetic smile he indicated that he had decided to save it for later. My wife immediately gave him one more. This confused him. At first he tried to push the second one behind the string as well, but then he changed his mind. Or so it seemed, because the next moment he was again unsure what to do.

My wife pulled the banana out of his hands, peeled it, broke it in two and placed the two halves back in his hands. Now he had no choice. Holding one half in each hand, he proceeded to eat it with undisguised pleasure, taking bites off each half in turn. When he finished, he spent another joyful minute licking his fingers. Then he pulled the first banana from behind the string and contemplated it with a blissful smile. Finally, pushing it back, he announced, "Grrr, grrr, ek, ek, brrr," which probably meant that one must also think of the future.

As we got up to leave, the banana slipped into his trousers, slid down his trouser leg and ended up at his feet. My wife and I couldn't help laughing. After a brief hesitation the boy joined in and laughed with complete abandon, grateful for an opportunity to take part in a joyful occasion.

He picked up the banana and turned to the soldier. "Grr, brrr, ek, ek?" he asked, ponting across the courtyard. As soon as the soldier nodded approval, Uki rushed to the far corner and hid the banana behind a piece of timber. Then he rushed back, grabbed hold of our hands and began to pull us towards the exit.

The soldier suddenly spoke. "No parents," he said. "The house burned down. They died. Together with Uki's brother. And two little sisters."

"Where does he live?" asked my wife.

"Everywhere," the soldier replied. "Sometimes, if it isn't too cold, he spends the night here. He sleeps in temples, under stalls in the market."

We left to continue sightseing. But it soon became obvious that we had seen most of what there was to see. The boy's eagerness, too, was evaporating. He looked tired and bored. He was waiting for his reward so he could return to his chums. Unable to find any coins, we gave him a ten-rupee note. He grew pale, his whole body shook. He held the note up to our eyes and anxiously enquired, "Grrr, brrr, ek?"

Yes, we nodded, the banknote was his. He still couldn't bring himself to believe it. Yes, we insisted, he could keep the money, it was his. And to convince him that we meant it, we gave him one more ten-rupee note.

"Grrr, brrr, grrr?" he repeated, now completely confused.

Yes, we said, they were both his to keep. His face exploded in a mixture of joy and gratitude. Holding one note in each hand he raised them high and danced off across the square. He showed the trophy to his astonished friends. Milling around him, they followed him down the road, screaming and laughing, proudly explaining to everybody who cared to listen how much money Uki had earned. People smiled and patted the lucky boy on the head. He kept readjusting his cap so it wouldn't fall off.

Quietly, we mounted our bicycles and set off. About a mile out of town, halfway up a steep slope, we ran out of breath and dismounted. Ten minutes later, at the top of the hill, we turned round to take a parting look at Pathan.

Standing in the middle of the road a few yards behind us, exhausted, his face flushed with guilt and defiance, was the little deaf mute. He kept looking from one to the other, waiting to see if our disbelief would turn to delight or anger. He produced a gurgle of insecure laughter.

"Grrr, grrr, ga ga, ek, brrr," he tried to explain.

The entreating look in his eyes slowly gave way to sadness. He was exhausted, the curls sticking out from under his cap were soaked with sweat. Using every gesture we could think of, we tried to persuade him to return to Pathan. Kathmandu was too big, we said, he would get lost. We were leaving for India, and wouldn't be able to look after him.

All he could understand was that we were sending him back, rejecting him.

Suddenly his face lit up. He rushed towards me, took off his cap and, using it as a duster, started to clean my shoes. Then, crouching in front of my wife, he proceeded to clean her sandals. Finally, turning the cap inside out, he began to polish the chrome parts of our bicycles.

"Sorry," we said. "You must go back."

We lept on our bikes and rode off. The relentless patter of little feet behind us finally softened our hearts. The boy must have known this would happen. We waited for him to catch up. As he did so, his legs gave way under him and he collapsed in the dust. He had no strength left, except to gurgle happily, "Grrr, brrr, ek."

I lifted him onto the crossbar and we set off towards Kathmandu. He swivelled his head round to look at me. His eyes were filled with relief and gratitude, but also with something that shocked me: something close to pure love. Once again he produced a gurgle of happy laughter.

Our intention was to take him to Kathmandu, show him the sights, buy him lunch and then, towads the evening, take him back to Pathan. But his joy at being in a big city was so great that we decided to let him stay the night. We took him to our hotel. We ran a bath for him, removed his clothes and lifted him into the tub. At first he was frightened and made a frantic attempt to climb out, but then he slowly calmed down and began to enjoy the new experience. Before long he was screaming with joy and splashing water all over the bathroom.

We took him to the nearest market and bought him a new shirt, a pair of trousers and soft leather sandals. His face assumed an expression of solemn dignity, his posture became rigid, unnatural. He felt a stranger to himself in his new outfit. As the shop owner flung his old clothes onto a heap of rubbish in the corner, Uki objected with a vehement "Grrr, brrr, ek, ek."

He rolled his old shirt and trousers into a bundle and firmly pressed them against his chest. "Ga, ga, brrr, grrr," he muttered. The miraculous world in which he had found himself was beginning to frighten him. His old clothes were the only link with his past, the only reminder of the familiar world he had left behind.

Towards the evening we took him to a Chinese restaurant. At first he refused to believe that the steaming dishes placed in front of us were real; he carefully prodded each with his fingers. As my wife and I began to eat, he remained convinced that the dishes had been put there for us alone. It was only after my wife piled some food onto his plate that he found enough courage to pick up his spoon.

Once he started to eat, however, there was no stopping him. Awkwardly holding the unwieldy spoon the way one normally holds a knife, he carried the food from the plate to his mouth in

71

a zig-zag fashion, with his mouth an elusive target that he missed more often than not. It wasn't long before he had noodles and gravy stuck all over his face, new shirt and trousers. Halfway through his third helping he suddenly became tired. His head sank onto the table. Without letting go of the spoon, he fell asleep.

We carried him to the hotel, took off his clothes, washed his face and hands, and put him to bed. He slept like a log. In the middle of the night he woke up. "Ga, ga, grrr, grrr, ek," he said, deeply alarmed. He had no idea where he was. His little fingers began to explore the surroundings. As they encountered my arm, they paused for a moment, then carried on. They found my wrist, my forefinger, my thumb. After some hesitation, they wrapped themselves firmly round the thumb. His face moved closer, I could feel his warm breath, still smelling of Chinese dinner. "Ek, ek, grrr, grrr," he muttered into my ear, relieved.

In the morning we took him sightseeing. We showed him the royal palace. Three garishly decorated elephants waddled out through the main gate and were led down the road. Uki screamed with delight. We had to follow the elephants for ten minutes. As we strolled through the centre of Kathmandu, he rushed about as if possessed, jumping up and down, throwing his arms in the air, pointing out this and that, laughing, explaining, wondering. In no time at all it was he who was showing us the sights of Kathmandu.

We hired a rikshaw. As the driver boldly maneuvered his garish vehicle through the crowd, Uki shouted and egged him on; he jerked and thrashed about as if having a fit, it was hard work trying to keep him from falling off. He gurgled, wheezed and laughed: the world, the wonderful world revolved around him like a magic roundabout. He was the happiest boy alive.

He stayed another night.

The following morning we cycled out of town to visit the Monkey Temple. The golden dome impressed Uki so deeply that he fell silent, gazing at it for almost ten minutes. He found the monkeys amusing, but as soon as one slipped away from the group and scuttled towards him, he screamed and flew into my arms. He was glad when we reached the bicycles we had left at the foot of the hill.

"Grrr, brrr, ek," he said as I lifted him onto the crossbar.

Skirting Kathmandu, we reached a dusty road leading south. There was no sign from Uki that he recognized it, or that he knew we were taking him back to Pathan. It was only when we entered the narrow alleyways that he began to recognize familiar landmarks. He seemed surprised, and delighted, that the old world was still there, unchanged. As we reached the market square, he spotted a group of his friends.

"Grrr, brrr, ek!" he exploded, frantically waving his arms. The children recognized him and rushed towards us, screaming a joyous welcome. By the time we dismounted, we were completely surrounded. The children wanted to touch Uki's new shirt and trousers, to stroke his sandals. I was reminded of Uki's behaviour in the Chinese restaurant; he, too, had to touch the dishes before he could believe they were real. He was pleased by his friends' admiration. Written all over his face was pride, a sense of achievement. But there wasn't a shade of conceit in his manner, he remained friendly and warm.

Then, with a sense of urgency, he embarked on a lengthy explanation. "Grrr, brrr, ek, ek, brrr," he burbled in an endless stream. He waved his arms about as if trying to draw in the air all the wonders he had seen, elephants, monkeys, palaces, everything, everything ...

Cautiously, we mounted our bikes and pedalled off across the square. We were stopped by a heart-rending cry. A moment later Uki was at my side, tugging at my trousers, trying to make me dismount. He stared at me with complete disbelief. He rushed to my wife and tried to pull her off the bike. He

73

returned to me, gripped the handlebars and deftly pulled himself up onto the crossbar. He wanted to stay with us, go with us back to Kathmandu, anywhere.

"Ek, brrr grrr grrr," he pleaded.

I tried to dislodge him, but he refused to let go. All his strength had concentrated in his little fingers. I finally managed to wrest one of his hands off the handlebars, but no sooner did I start with the second than the first one was back, gripping the handlebars even harder.

Then, unexpectedly, he subsided – like a taut football suddenly going soft. He felt silent and his hands slipped off the handlebars. He did not object when I put him down on the ground. For a while he stood there, surrounded by his puzzled friends, and stared at his feet. Then, slowly, he raised his head and looked me straight in the eyes.

Was this really the end?

As soon as he knew that it was, he lowered his head again, turned and walked across the square towards the wall of the nearest building. When he reached it, he sat down next to it and, leaning his head against it, turned his face away from us. There he remained, motionless.

My wife walked to the nearest stall and bought a bunch of bananas. She took them over to Uki and placed them into his lap. He opened his eyes and uttered a tired, unwilling "Grrr, brrr, ga ga, ek." Then he closed his eyes again. I reached down and pressed a hundred-rupee note into his hand. He looked at it without interest. His hand remained lifeless, the banknote slid to the ground.

I tickled him under the chin. I wanted to cheer him up, see him smile. He refused to look at me. Just before we left the square I turned around.

Leaning against the wall, he looked like a hostage executed by a firing squad.

Translated by the author

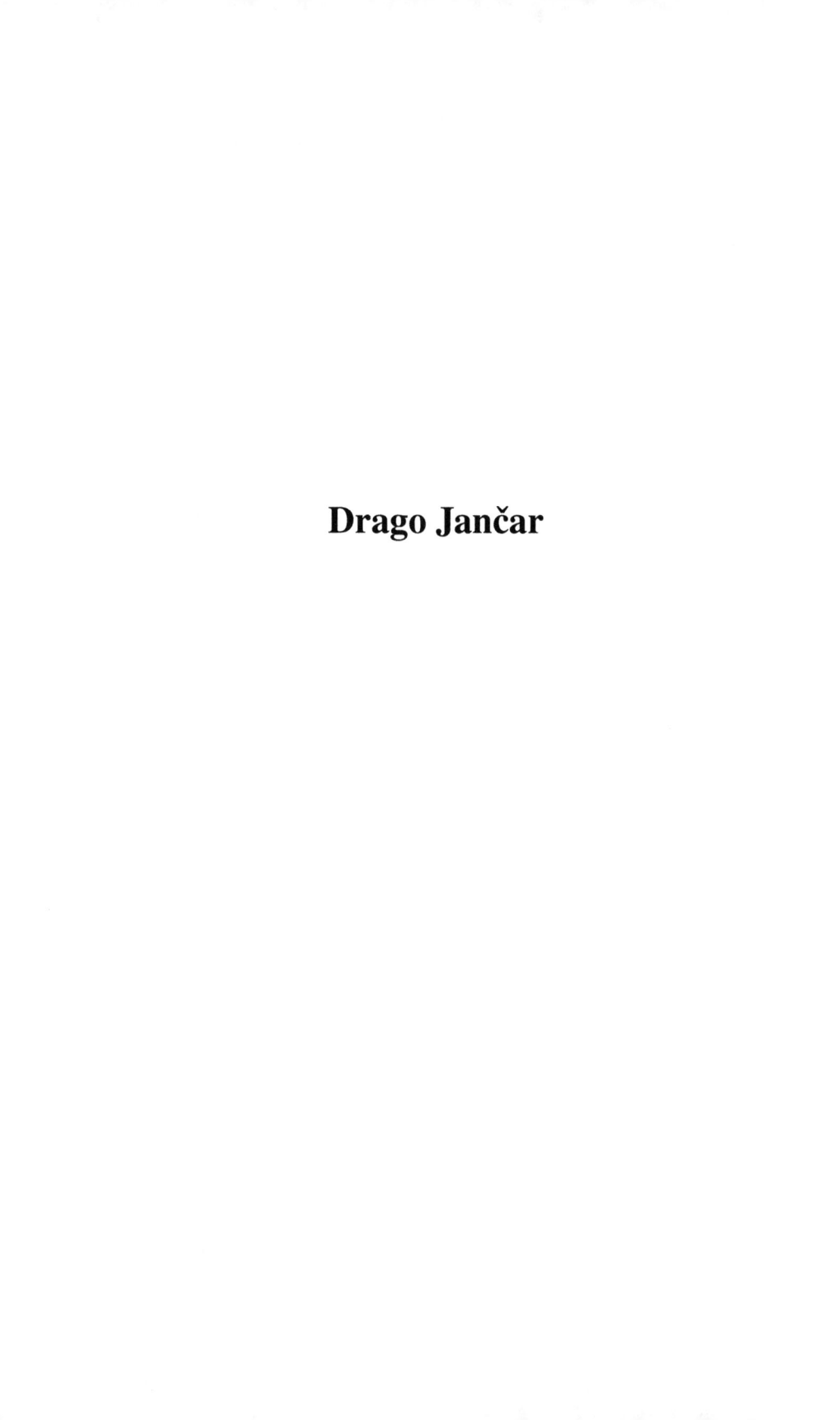

Drago Jančar

Drago Jančar, *born 1948 in Maribor, Slovenia, is one of the best-known Slovenian writers at home and abroad. He studied law, worked as journalist, editor and freelance writer. In 1985, he stayed in the USA as a Fulbright fellow, in 1988 he lived in Germany. As President of the Slovenian PEN Center (1987–91) he was engaged in the advance of democracy in Slovenia and Yugoslavia. His novels and short stories have been translated into several European languages and published in Europe and the USA. In 1993, he was awarded the Prešeren Prize, the highest Slovenian literary award. In 1994, in Arnsbeg, Germany, he won the European Short Story Award. He lives in Ljubljana. His best-known novels are Northern lights, Mocking Desire, and Katarina, Peacock and the Jesuit. His best known plays are The Great Brilliant Waltz and Hallstat. He is the author of highly praised award-winning collections of essays.*

ULTIMA CREATURA

Drago Jančar

Had Franc Rutar, on a humid afternoon long past, not fixed his gaze on the large letters of a book the woman sitting next to him was holding on her knees, everything would have ended much better. He would not have experienced the horrible things, which, even years later, when he thought of them with a mixture of painful discomfort and fear, appeared like images from a bad dream. From moments between sleep and wakefulness. But he knew that this was not a dream, although everything had happened in a large, distant city, the pictures of which, just like dreams, were coming into his life from the TV screen. In the middle of a humid afternoon he was rushing into the underground, and the god he met there was black and dreadful. At least, he claimed he was God, and Franc Rutar recognized him as such, although then and even now he thought he had been somebody else, God's dark antithesis. God does not think of such cheap tricks, he does not seek weak points in the weak moments of settled people in such a way. Franc Rutar was more and more certain of this, the more distant the unpleasant event became.

Sales representative, Franc Rutar, was an avaricious reader. Although numbers and letters often danced before his tired eyes, he could not help swallowing every single word and letter that happened to be in his field of vision. He was one of those people who, in waiting rooms, in buses or just anywhere read from newspapers and books that were not theirs. They cannot help glancing at the front page of the paper somebody else holds in their hands. Many do it out of laziness or tightness, some out of thievish impulses: they read over the owner's shoulder, and since they know very well how annoying this is, they always look away just before they are caught red handed, and start looking through the window or at the tips of their shoes. Some of these readers never even think of the fact that they are actually stealing somebody else's property with their eyes, letter by letter, like bits of a female body, like bread from a table. Franc Rutar could not complain of a scarcity of his foreign trade and other reading material. However, reading the papers and books other people field in their hands became his uncontrollable passion. By doing it, he again and again tested his exact mind; Franc Rutar was a man with an exact mind and perfect memory. He immediately connected the dancing titles and fragments of pages into rounded logical wholes; a sports report was never mixed up with a political one. Anyone who has an orderly head can apprehend the order of the world, and mistakes cannot happen. His greatest pleasure was to catch a glimpse of a crossword puzzle; he could feel pins and needles at the sudden challenge and risk. He could test the speedy operation of his brain, which was one of his greatest assets in concluding risky editorial deals; rapid considerations, swift decisions. With brisk calculations, tossing the words around, he managed to solve the puzzles between two stops. Franc Rutar was of the opinion, according to his own beliefs, that he was one of the supreme achievements of the Creation.

On the very first day he proved this fact to the colleague from his company with whom he had come to New York. After a few hours of his stay in the metropolis he understood the mathematics of Manhattan streets, finding them no more diffi- cult than the average crossword puzzle. Thanks to him they were able to quickly carry out sophisticated foreign trade deals. On the third day he felt at home in this human anthill of business, he beamed at his friend's praise; that was the famous dexterity and ingenuity of Franc Rutar's mind, he did not lack reasons for satisfaction. Not even after he had, on the third afternoon of his stay – it was a stuffy afternoon, saturated with ocean humidity – appeased his hunger with cheap fried chicken in a fast food restaurant. He contentedly sat on a subway train, which was to take him somewhere towards Battery Park. where he wanted to take a walk around Wall Street. He was in New York, his business settled, his stomach full, the world was high and life beautiful. But when the world is at its highest, the fall from the top is deepest.

He looked around him for an open newspaper. He was going to test his impeccable English in the risky game of connecting fragments into logical wholes, between two stops. He was about to get up to step behind the back of a man holding a folded paper in one hand and clutching onto the swaying handle with the other, when a better, for the moment of con- tentment more appropriate opportunity arose. A beautiful black girl sat down next to him, actually a woman, a girl still, but a woman at the same time. She opened a book on her lap, and soon got absorbed in reading. There was no need to stretch his neck, no need to stand behind somebody's back and look over a shoulder, luxurious reading was right there, immobile, open above the round, chocolate brown knees. The letters were large, so he could easily follow the text written in simple English. The task was almost too simple. But he had just come from lunch, warm matter mixed with fried Kentucky chicken was lazily and happily flowing through his body. He abandoned himself to the large letters and the rocking train rushing into the black underground.

He suddenly felt excited and wide awake. The text resting on top of the naked chocolate knees, nicely cooled in the tiled subway in the middle of a stuffy day above, was shocking. Franc Rutar had never read anything like it, at least not in a train: a young woman was just about to lie, half way through the left page of the book, with an older man, actually an old man, as it soon became clear. It was written in the first person, the narrator was the woman. She locked the door of her flat behind her, she was undoing the buttons on his shirt, at the beginning of the following page she leaned towards his neck and with intoxicated desire was smelling his aged skin.

Franc Rutar deeply resented any frivolity, temptations of the flesh, and contacts with strangers were in opposition to the order in his mind. He avoided all the things that some of his colleagues openly looked for on business trips. He once looked at the women in shop windows in Hamburg, but to spend his hard-earned money on them never crossed his mind, not even in a dream. However, before the impulse reached his mind, he was all in a trembling frenzy he had never experienced before. Was it the humid day or was it the inconceivable fact that the young woman, who was not even a woman yet, was sitting next to him and reading such things? Also the sudden decision that he would not get off and finish the story in his mind, but that he would, on the contrary, actually read the thing on the knees, was spontaneous; it was not the product of consideration, but of some unknown impulse in his brain and body. Voraciously he read the next page, on which the senseless erotic scene continued, and he could only conclude that the girl in the book was either intoxicated, crazy or in love in some strange way. He waited impatiently for the slow reader to turn the page. He had long moments at his disposal to take a better

80

look at her. He saw her moving lips. Moist, red lips. He missed his stop, but she still had not turned the page. She was moving her knees. A naive girl, he thought, she is embellishing her life with cheap romances in large type. She must work in one of those department stores, wrapping up clothes with awkward fingers all day long. He thought he would get off after all. At that moment the round chocolate knees moved. She crossed her legs and turned the page at the same time. Everything happened simultaneously, for a long moment her hot thigh pressed against his with such strength that something rushed from his brain and his organ into his chest at the same time, whizzed towards his heart and there, above the top of his stomach, this hollow something settled down and refused to dissolve. The letters started twinkling before his eyes.

He did not get off. He heard the roaring of the train rushing somewhere into the underground. She lifted the covers, and through the mist of his stunned eyes he saw on the fluorescent red cover the hollow between the woman's breasts, a broken necklace above them, crystal drops of sweat or water. The title of the book he read in a split second was: *The World Is Full of Married Men*. Whatever was holding a grip on his heart loosened, and what lay hollow on top of his stomach dissolved. He flinched, and his exact brain started working with computer speed, so that something cracked with fatigue a few times just under the arch of his skull. This here, he thought, this here is a set up. This girl, his precise mind continued, is sitting on the subway just for this. The letters are large so that somebody else can read them, under the book, chocolate knees. Yet, his mind crackled in an effort: Why? It is done differently for money. Because, his quick brain answered, because the girl wants to experience exactly this. She is black, discriminated against, frustrated. Where else can she find a businessman, an older man, even an aged man, if not on the subway? She might become his mistress; it is common knowledge that such men in their most secret dreams want unpredictable events, young mulatto girls. At this conclusion he again became pleased with himself, although not a bit less excited; if he had been merely excited a few minutes before, and before that only pleased, then now he was both, excited and pleased. Excited flesh, contented mind. She had sat down next to him, not somebody else. It was true that his belly was growing and that he had a monkish tonsure on his head, although it was not showing. He must still have been immensely more interesting than the old man described with such passion on the strange pages of the book resting on the knees. I'll get off, he decided, where she gets off, and let happen what must. One can, after all, take a ride back the very next moment. He was astonished by such a brisk decision. If she asks for money, he thought, and prolonged the thought into a consideration, I can think about that on the spot. He was pleased with himself, the decision originated from his reason and contentment, partly from excitement.

The train was at that moment scurrying towards Brooklyn. We're traveling under the water, he thought, what an adventure, up there is the huge, dark mass of the bridge we know from films; he, Franc Rutar is riding underneath it, a black girl is seducing him. He was looking at her knees, the rim of her skirt above them, he was touching her ribs under the light blouse with his elbow, his gaze fixed on her dark skin, he was traveling into her. Derma, his brain quickly said, five letters from a crossword puzzle. What's the matter with me, he thought, where am I going?

She stood up and smoothed her skirt. He stepped to the door, close behind her. He straightened his tie and thought it would soon be undone, just like the one on the pages of the book she was now clutching under her sweaty arm. On the platform she looked straight into his eyes, he felt the look penetrated deeply.

No, there was no doubt about it. His heart was pounding. All he needed to do now was find the courage to address her. It would not happen without speaking. He was rapidly searching for words. He would speak in a muffled way, slightly through the nose, to conceal his Slovene accent. Her hips were swaying in front of his eyes, the light from the street approached and a house with a shabby facade above it. He would speak loudly, so that she would not be able to hear the hammering of his heart. Before they reached the top he had found the right words. Interesting book, isn't it? he said. What? she laughed with her pearl white teeth, What? The book, he said through his nose, with a deep voice. Oh yes, the book, she said and laughed brightly. He youthfully jumped over a few steps, now they were in the street. Again he was at a loss for words in the empty space in his skull. He found them. May I buy you a coffee? he said with an even deeper voice. I could buy you one, she said, so that he did not know whether it was an invitation or an ironic refusal. If you came this far, the suddenly determined brain said, then go all the way. Or maybe it said nothing. The sales representative, Franc Rutar, probably because of every-thing unexpected that had happened in his life was left without the brain which had helped him to conclude business transac-tions and solve crossword puzzles so successfully. If he had still had the brain, he would have seen that he was accompany-ing a young black woman at a fast pace along a horribly shabby New York street, jumping over heaps of rubbish and avoiding bodies lying on the sidewalks. Through black people sitting on steps, through their faces he pushed his way after her, after her all the time, through a door into a dark hall. From there new stairs led high up, between wooden walls close together. Through a narrow corridor, up the steel stairs he walked close behind her, with no eyes, with the smell of her derma in his nostrils, with his sweat pouring through his hair, dripping from his forehead and slithering into his shirt; with the smell of rotten wood which was covered in places with peeling wallpaper.

At the top she opened a door, then another. They were in a small room. Children's chatter was coming from the street, and tenants' echoing calls from balconies and windows, and wild musical confusion from different directions. In the corner, in semi darkness stood a shabby couch with a metal spring sticking from it. He loosened his tie, although he still expected her to do it before undoing the buttons on his shirt, as it was done in the book. Sweat was pouring from his face, his heart was pounding crazily, partly because of the run up the stairs. In a corner of his mind, not the one with swift and precise thoughts, but the one with a premonition, something said something; he could not discern what exactly it said, it did not run along the folds, it did not switch itself on, and even if it had, if he could have discerned what that something was which had said something, and what it had said, it would have been too late.

The dark girl sat on the couch in the dark part of the room, she looked emptily at the wall, opened her mouth and started screaming. Surprised, he looked at the disfigured face of the being sitting there, and he could not understand why, why she was sitting there screaming; he thought of somehow stopping that open mouth, from which a high, monotonous shriek was coming. Excuse me, he said, this is a misunderstanding, he said, I'm sorry. I'll hit her, he thought, why is she screaming, I haven't done anything to her, I'll hit her, he thought.

She did not scream long, towards the end not even very loudly. The door opened immediately. A young black man with a massive gold chain around his neck walked in. He was chewing negligently. What's happening here? he said, mumbling the question rather indistinctly, and it must have meant what Franc Rutar had already understood: he was her protector. He wanted

84

to rape me, the girl said, as she would have said it's four in the afternoon. The chewing man looked at him accusingly and with surprise. Who? he asked. She pointed at Franc Rutar with her finger: Him.

At that moment his brain finally recognized what was coming from the vast premonition area. He was trapped. He thought he was a stupid, contented man, whose brain worked stupidly, following stupid instincts. Suddenly he did not understand how he happened to be there at all. I'm, he said, by chance ... It did not sound convincing. He was dripping with cold sweat, and he felt a strange emptiness spreading in his head, something completely unspecified, something like nothing. I'm sorry, he said, I'm sorry, and took a step towards the door. The young black man pressed his back against it. It was impossible to leave the place just like that. If muggers stop you in the street, his memory whispered to him, have a ten dollar bill ready in your pocket. Give it to them immediately, without wasting any words. He reached into his breast pocket and discovered with relief that the money was still there. Franc Rutar was a careful man, ready for anything, even for being stopped in the street by hooligans. But he was not in a street. He was in an unknown flat, in an unknown part of town, the exit from this dive was blocked by a young man who was chewing and playing with the chain on his chest. He never even looked at the banknote, he opened the door and called somebody. Immediately two other men walked in, they obviously could not have been very far away. One of them took over the post by the door; the other, a tall and slender middle aged man, walked around the room. He was wearing a white linen jacket, he exchanged a few sentences with the girl, who was still sitting by the protruding spring; he spoke Spanish. He then turned to Franc Rutar, who with eyes full of hope was following his movements and speech. He said they would call the police. Yes, the sales representative whispered, yes, the police. Everybody went quiet, the young and the tall one exchanged a long look. No, Franc Rutar said, no need to call. Sir, the young man with the chain said, Sir, your tie is undone. He lifted his chin and fastened his tie so tightly that he was left breathless. This doesn't make any sense, Franc Rutar thought, any sense. The tall man offered him a seat by the girl. He sank into himself and lowered his eyes. The tall man walked around the room and asked the girl questions, she answered with shrieking, bickering screams, the nauseating screech of the imagined girl with chocolate derma. The mumbling young man joined in the conversation, only the third one stood silently by the door. Oh my God, the sales rep thought, they are fighting for the prey. He was made to stand by the wall and raise his arms so that they were able to search him. Then he had to empty his pockets and since there was no table, put everything on the floor. The young man with the chain suddenly became very angry. The wallet was not among the articles on the floor. He shouted something incomprehensible, he turned round as if dancing, and hit Franc Rutar on the neck with his half open fist so hard that he instantly collapsed on the floor. At once he handed him his wallet. The white jacket asked him something. He did not understand, he did not know what to answer. He grabbed his hair and shook his poor head and breathed his sweet breath into him. He could not, he did not understand, he did not know what was happening. Oh my dear Mamma, he muttered to himself, my dear Mummy, look what's happening to Franci. The girl opened his briefcase and emptied it on the couch. With clawing movements she scratched among his papers, put his pocket calculator and his glasses between the covers of the book; the tall one took the case. This is horrible, he thought, horrible what is happening to Franc far away from home; if his wife knew; he thought of everybody he loved who were so far away. But, what had happened so far was nothing in comparison with what followed.

86

He had to take his clothes off. He folded them on the couch. The third man, the one who was standing by the door without speaking, pulled a knife from his pocket, opened it, moved the blade down his neck. Then he lowered it to his organ. He'll cut it off, Franc Rutar realized, and put it in my mouth. The girl was frantically feeling his clothes. They were pushing him around the room and screaming over one another. Her shrieks were piercing his ears, the membrane of the tympanum, penetrating into the soft tissue of the brain. Somebody switched on the radio, somebody drank from a can, pouring beer all over him. The noise was terrible. Then for a moment there was silence in the room, through the veil of mist he saw a tall black man in a dark jacket approach. He came very close and quietly whispered into his ear, so that his head hollowly echoed with his breath and words. I'm your God, he said, do you understand? Franc nodded. Repeat, he said, repeat: who am I? God, he said, my God. Your great God, the tall black man said, his head was just below the ceiling when he stood up, Franc Rutar was lying on the floor, the small head of the great God high above. My great God, he said loudly, as many times as he could. He heard his voice getting lost in the empty space, coming back with an echo, as if he had been speaking in a huge hall.

He was forced to lie on the floor and put his hands on his nape. They walked around the room and again talked loudly. They stumbled over him, somebody sat on top of him for a moment. Now... he thought... the knife. Or... a blow on the head. He could see his corpse floating under Brooklyn Bridge, the shadow of the giant bridge above, below, under the water, the rattling of the subway. He remembered he used to know a prayer, he started moving his trembling lips, pressed against the dirty wooden floor: Our Father who art in Heaven. The clamor was far away, the musical chaos was coming from yards and balconies. Darkness fell over his eyes, voices and words, screams and slams of the door became intermingled. His body became insensitive, black shadows danced around him. He shrank into a little boy being put into a cauldron and danced around. Now they'll cut me into pieces, the dreaming boy in the bed thought, and they'll put me into that cauldron, into that big vessel Mamma used to cook jam in. Then he knew he was asleep, and that he saw his white body floating under the bridge, in its large shadow. The belly was slightly swollen, the tumult of the city coming from afar. The tumult changed into a shrill, hissing noise. Steam was hissing from a pipe. Again he heard Spanish words from a distance, then they became Latin; was it the tall black man in the white jacket speaking? He could hear two words quite distinctly; from a crossword puzzle, said his brain, which was obviously still working, from a difficult puzzle. Ultima creatura, he said. Ultima creatura. He rapidly placed the letters in the squares, his inner eye saw the squares and the two emerging words. Do these black gods speak Latin? he thought with surprise; there is a certain logic in it, he thought, gods always speak Latin, is that what the black God is telling him?

For a long time he listened to the hissing of the steam, penetrating his awakening consciousness together with calls from the distance, from the street, probably from the balconies in the neighboring buildings. He opened his eyes. It was dark in the room, a ray of light from the street fell at an angle onto his white body. In the empty flat, only then did he realize there was no glass in the windows, it smelt of humidity, decaying wallpaper, rotten wood. All his senses functioned: smell, sight, hearing, the aching body. There were holes in the floor, his clothes lay crumpled on it, in the corner a white, slovenly pile, the shirt, that was the shirt. The tie hung on the spring sticking from the pierced couch. He dressed. Feeling through the darkness he descended the steep stairs of the empty house.

He arrived at his hotel towards morning. He told no one what had happened to Franc. To his friend who knocked on the door he said he had been robbed in a park. He did not find it necessary to explain anything. When the friend looked at him with surprise through the half open door, looked at the deep scar running from the ear towards the mouth, he closed the door and lay on the bed. Explain nothing. Say nothing. Even think nothing. He did not leave the room until he left for home. He lay on the bed and lovingly looked at the plane ticket and the passport, which had been, on advice from the homeland, left locked in the hotel safe. The representative Franc Rutar was a careful and sensible man. At least he still had a tiny reason for satisfaction.

For many years he dreamt he was being put into that big vessel his Mamma used to cook jam in. He floated in the shadow of a huge bridge, with his belly white and swollen. In an empty room a black god leaned over him and breathed unknown horrible words into his ears. When the silhouette of an unknown city or bridge appeared on TV, he switched the set off and had a fight with his wife, who could not understand it. He always had it his way, he could not stand humiliation. He avoided young mulatto girls from department stores. Luckily, there were not many in his country. Never again did he read over somebody else's shoulder or tackle a crossword puzzle.

A few years after the trip to New York, on a winter night, by the fence of his suburban house, he knocked down a drunken tramp who had asked him for some change. Creature, he shouted, creature, and kicked the rasping heap on the ground. The incident was reported in the local paper, which discretely published only his initials: F. R. That was all, nothing else happened apart from the things that happen to any of us.

Translated by Lili Potpara

Milan Kleč

Milan Kleč, born 1954, is a prose writer and playwright, mostly author of numerous collections of short stories and radio plays for children. His best known books are Hair, Balance, Bicycle thieves, Still alone, and A very good man and honest friend. He was awarded Prešeren Fund prize for literature. His work has been translated into a number of languages.

ŠKILAN

Milan Kleč

Yesterday I knew absolutely nothing about Škilan. So I must really have taken something to heart, since I am writing these lines now. I became interested in him by accident, on the bus on my way home. I was very self-absorbed, so I was even more surprised that something had managed to catch my attention. Two passengers sitting in front of me, whom I did not know, talked about a certain Škilan, who apparently had an accident while picking bilberries. They laughed out loud, and the one who obviously knew the Škilan case better added that Škilan could only pick bilberries with the help of a ladder. I was not sure whether I had heard him correctly or not, of course I never checked; the mere thought that apparently somewhere there was a man, as far as I was concerned his name could well be Škilan, and that that man had to pick bilberries with a ladder, was enough for me. I could picture a little man, running around the forest with a ladder, putting it up every bilberry bush, and then climbing up, picking the fruit and scurrying back down, placing the fruit in a little basket. However, one can easily miss a ladder-rung and alas ! an accident. I could very well visualize this Škilan, how he reached out for a bilberry, the ladder had

93

swung in the wind, or else the shrub was rather weak; I could see him fall and then crawl home from where he was taken away and put in plaster. I trusted this Škilan completely, although of course I did not know why. The thing itself was something; I mean, that after a long time I could trust somebody, regardless of whether he had to pick bilberries with a ladder or not. I thought a lot about him. I somehow could not sleep at night, and I did not know why. I got up and smoked. And I kept switching the bed-lamp on and off. I sat for some time, and then I walked. I also looked through the window. I breathed deeply, but not because I felt uneasy. I felt good, and I did not mind the slight excitement at all. The weather was also rather warm. I saw the same clouds in the moonlight. I cannot say I thought of anything in particular. I did not feel the least lonely, although I used to in similar situations. It was sometimes very irritating. Also, in the mornings I never changed my routine. Actually, it was not quite like this. I do not know why, but all of a sudden I dug out an old suitcase. I used to travel with it, and every year we must have looked more and more bizarre. I recalled nice moments as I was dusting it. A pleasant old suitcase, and I looked into its empty contents. I, on the contrary, was full. That is why I knew I had to fill it up with something. Although I had no intention of travelling. Slowly I walked around the room, and started filling it up. I found half a loaf of bread, liver pate, some salami and a few swings of wine. That was enough. I wrapped everything together in a cloth, put it in the suitcase and closed it. It was full. It stood more upright. And then it was dawn. A beautiful morning was to be expected, as I had mentioned before, and a beautiful day. I put on strong shoes, and donned a jacket, although it was not appropriate for the season; underneath I wore my only suit. The white shirt was a little yellow, but I could do nothing about it. I locked the room and soon reached the fields. I really did not know where I was going. I was drawn somewhere, as people will say for the moments when we blindly follow some instinct, and as soon as I thought of this I at the same time knew I was not that kind of a person. Or maybe I was becoming such a person. I met some children, girls and boys, who where the only people out, and I asked them where Škilan lived. And as children do, they, half seriously, half jokingly pointed their fingers somewhere towards the distance. I walked through many fields, I crossed a river and forests and jumped over a railway. Villages passed me by. And one house was really shifted more into the forest. The house or Škilan? Both together. And I reached that house. A small house. I recalled Škilan picking bilberries. I actually noticed some ladders, one of them was broken, and it could well have been the one that caused the accident. I knocked. At first nobody answered, so I knocked harder, when something moved inside. I heard a voice and I remembered he had broken bones and probably had difficulty walking, so I simply walked in and then further into the house. I saw him. He was just getting ready to stand up on crutches. "Are you Škilan?" I asked him just to say something. As if I had known I had come to the right place. Just to do something, he nodded. He really was a man one could trust. At first glance. So small, and so warm. "How's it going?" I asked him, just like that. "So so," he answered. Then we were quiet for some moments, but not because we were at a loss for words. Škilan sat down with enormous difficulty and asked: "Did you come here to die?" I nodded, wanting to meet his eyes, but he pointed his finger at the room on his left, where I went with my suitcase, and where, at a small table, I have just written this.

Translated by Lili Potpara

Feri Lainšček

Feri Lainšček, *born in 1959 in Prekmurje, north-eastern Slovenia, is best known for his novels, published by various Slovenian publishing houses. He also writes poems, plays, and books for children. He has received numerous awards, among them the Prešeren Fund award for the novel Ki jo je megla prinesla (Brought Along by the Mist), Best Novel of the Year Award for the novel Namesto koga roža cveti (Instead of Whom the Flower Blooms), Children's Book of the Year Award for a collection of fairytales, and many others. Three of his novels have been filmed.*

TALES OF THE HEART

Feri Lainšček

AGNES AND THE ANGEL

Near the village of Greatwater, there once stood a mighty castle with powerful walls and high turrets. A count and a countess lived in the castle with their only daughter; they had no male heir. Their daughter's name was Agnes and she was beautiful, well-mannered and wise. All the same, her mother and father were never satisfied with her. The worst of it was that she was taking her time finding a husband and they feared that the county seat would be left with no descendants at all.

When Agnes was a small girl, one of the castle maidens showed her a hidden pool beneath the source from which the small lake around the castle bubbled up. In the early morning light, angels used to come and bathe in this water that was as clear and pure as any water the human eye has ever seen. Whoever was fortunate enough to tiptoe to the edge of the pool could secretly watch the angels swimming there. They laid their wings down in the dewy grass and rushed into the pool and splashed the water far and wide. They swam in the deep water, turned somersaults and played with the fish who were overcome with joy. But if the angels ever sensed a human being close at hand, they quickly put on their wings and flew away.

"When the time comes to choose a husband," Agnes said, "he must be exactly like one of these angels."

"You shall never find a beauty as pure as that in this world," the castle maidens laughed, "even if you search for the rest of your days."

"Well then," the stubborn Agnes replied, "I shall have to marry an angel."

Although she was only a child when she made this vow, it was etched in her heart and she was never able to forget it. Indeed, she often wondered how she could approach the angels without frightening them and making them fly away. She imagined that one of the angels would notice her and be unable to look away from her womanly charms.

The old castle gardener had been watching Agnes all these years and knew of her secret desire. He believed he knew a way she could fulfill her dream. "If you sneak up to the pool while the angels are swimming and hide one set of wings, one angel will no longer be able to fly away," the gardener whispered into her ear. "And if you submerge the angel's wings into the pool, they will grow heavy with water, and the angel will always have to stay by your side," he added. "But think long and hard before you do such a thing. An angel who must always remain on earth will grow sad from time to time and you will always have to worry that his heart might break from bitterness."

Agnes thought about it all night long and found herself unable to resist the temptation of the gardener's idea.

Morning after morning, she hid behind a flowering bush beside the pool and waited for the angels to come. When they finally descended, the most beautiful among them laid down his shiny wings. Agnes rushed forward and grabbed the wings and flung them into the water. Suddenly the water began to whirl in a tight eddy and the pool was filled with bubbles. In the confusion, most of the angels grabbed their wings and flew straight up to the sky. Only the most beautiful among them remained, searching in vain for his wings. Finally he sat on a rock with his arms hanging limply at his sides and struggled to catch his breath.

"I did that," Agnes whispered to him when he finally lifted his gaze, "because I could no longer resist the desire in my heart. But I promise you that my love will never waver and that I will do everything I can to make your life on earth beautiful.«

The angel silently accepted Agnes' extended hand and went with her to the castle. Her mother and father were delighted since they had long since given up hope that their daughter would marry. During the next seven days, they prepared a wedding celebration the likes of which had never been seen in the land. The old count gave his daughter's groom the keys to the castle and passed on the jeweled sword which had always traveled in the hands of the family and its descendents. All of this meant that the heavenly angel had become earthly royalty and was now the master of the wide fertile realm around Greatwater.

When the young count went to survey his estate, he discovered that all his subjects had to pay taxes and bring most of their harvest to the castle granaries. This made him sad, which troubled the young countess who loved him and feared that his heart might break from bitterness. On the very same day, new laws were entered into the ledgers, proclaiming that the count's subjects need no longer pay taxes. As far as the castle granaries were concerned, the count's subjects might contribute whatever they deemed appropriate.

Not long afterwards, the young count went to see the villages and markets in the realm and discovered that there was poverty and hardship around each and every corner. This made him sad and he persuaded the countess that the gates to the castle should be open night and day so that the poor might come to eat when they were hungry or sleep if they had no roof over their heads. And so the castle at Greatwater was transformed into a refuge for vagabonds and starving families who hadn't enough to feed their children.

On Sunday, the newlyweds went to visit the neighboring castle. The young count immediately noticed that in this district all were impoverished because the land on the estates was not sufficiently fertile and the valley had suffered from drought for many years in a row. The young count was filled with pity and the young countess, fearing for his tender heart, allowed him to give a part of their land to the neighboring castle.

And so they went on helping and giving to others who were in difficult straits. Because of this, people loved them and respected them more than ordinary people love and respect their lord. People from distant places heard about the compassionate and generous count and soon they came from far and wide to enjoy his mercy. Little by little, they took away all the wealth that had accumulated over the centuries in the realm of Greatwater until finally only the castle itself remained. But the young count and countess were not troubled by this at all. Agnes had always loved her angel more than anything else in the world and she took great care that he never felt sad.

When at last the two were left with no belongings at all, the young count and countess set out barefoot to discover the world. They enjoyed the freedom of travelers who wander with no destination in mind and only look forward to one carefree day after another. Everyone who met them could see that they were as happy and in love as few are lucky to be.

One day, their travels carried them to the main market in front of Blatograd where some thieves were being tried for their crimes. Among the accused were a Gypsy and his wife who had stolen into the castle at night and taken a handful of valuable gems from the crown of the king. Their crime was so great in the eyes of the judge that they could hope for no mercy even though they had seven little children who desperately gathered round them.

The young count, who in his traveling rags looked like an ordinary tramp, took pity on these frail and sickly children. Without thinking, he stepped before the judge and said: "I confess that it was I who stole the precious jewels from the crown of the king and I sold them to this Gypsy for a sausage and a pretzel. Therefore, I beg you to mete out the appropriate punishment to me and release this innocent father from his irons to tend to his poor and hungry children."

The judge was astonished by this confession and had no wish to believe it.

"In the king's chambers from which the gems were stolen, we also found the traces of a woman's bare foot prints," he reluctantly replied. "That means that there were two thieves and that it could only have been these minions who stand before me now. You have made up your confession because you pity their seven small children."

At that moment, the countess Agnes, dressed in rags like an ordinary tramp, stepped before the judge: "I confess that I was the second thief who stole these precious jewels and that we then sold them to this Gypsy for a sausage and a pretzel. Therefore, I beg you to mete out the appropriate punishment to me and release this innocent mother from her irons to tend to her poor and hungry children."

There was nothing left for the judge to do but release the Gypsy and his wife and take into custody the two vagabonds who had freely confessed to the crime. He sentenced them to death.

"Your love was the most beautiful thing I have ever known and, because of it, I am not sorry that I have lived as a man on this earth," the young count said to Agnes before he lowered his head on the executioner's block.

"Your goodness was the most beautiful thing that ever visited this earth and, because of it, I am not sorry that now I must die," replied the young countess as she lowered her head.

Soon after the cruel executioner had carried out his duty, Agnes was surprised to awaken in another world. Her young husband, once again wearing the wings of an angel, was by her side and smiled at her in greeting. She took the hand he extended to her and, although she could not feel the ground beneath her feet, she stood up. Fearing that she would fall, she let out a scream. "Flap your wings, my beloved angel!" her husband instructed her as he guided her out into the boundless sky and let her go. Agnes did flap her wings and discovered that she could easily follow along behind him. She too had become an angelic creature.

Many many years passed and the castle at Greatwater no longer stands.

All that remains is the tale that grandparents recount to their grandchildren about the good count and his loving countess. The little lake and the clear pool beneath the source also remain and it is said that the two sometimes return to bathe there. But nobody goes in the early morning to secretly watch them. Nobody would want to disturb their happiness and the eternal love that brought so much goodness to this place.

BEAUTIFUL ANGELICA

This story took place when Monastra was still a great market town and only the most well-to-do families lived in the city's large and beautiful houses. Angelica lived with her servants in a white villa at the end of the street. When they died, her mother and father had left her with such riches that she could have anything she desired without ever so much as lifting a finger. On top of her great wealth, destiny had granted her such striking beauty that the breath was taken away from all who laid eyes on her, and suitors bowed to the floor before her. But despite all of this, Angelica was always alone because no one seemed to suit her and she didn't care to share her wealth with anyone.

A young coachman named Layosh lived in a hut on the banks of the Raba River. In the morning, he carried fruits and vegetable to the market in Monastra and in the evening he brought the worn-out peasants back home. He was a handsome and pleasant young man who always had a nice word for everyone and that is why people liked him. Though he lived modestly and some days survived on bread alone, he never demanded high payment for his services. It was said that he inherited his warm heart from his father who was a Gypsy and who, when he died, had left the boy a coach and four horses. Layosh inherited his modesty from his mother who, though not a Gypsy herself, had loved a Gypsy and had been a Gypsy's wife. When she died, she had only a small copper vessel filled with perfume from the markets of Budapest to leave to her son. Wherever he went, he always wore the little vessel on a leather strap around his neck. He told anyone who asked that it gave him luck and meant more to him than anything else in the world.

One morning, the miller asked the young coachman to take him to the white villa at the end of the street to deliver a bag of his best wheat flour. Fate desired that Angelica would be in her garden at the time, having already been served breakfast by her servants. Layosh stared into her big brown eyes and was unable to remove his gaze. It seemed to him that this was the instant that a man experiences only once in life. His heart, beating wildly in his chest, confirmed this feeling. Angelica, who was already accustomed to the embarrassment she caused in others, laughed aloud and revealed her beautiful teeth which glittered in the sun like the purest pearls and blinded the young man.

Poor Layosh had no recollection afterward of how he left the garden and his horses had to lead the way the rest of the day. The young coachman was so bewitched that he looked right through the people he drove home and he forgot to take the money that they held out to him. All of his thoughts remained with the beauty in the garden. He racked his brains trying to figure out a way to see her again. During the night, he was unable to close his eyes for even an instant. Right before dawn, he was struck by an idea. He would go to the miller and buy a bag of the best wheat flour with the last of his meager savings. He would bring it in front of the white villa at the end of the street and when the beautiful young woman came into the garden, he would drive his coach right into the courtyard.

"We didn't order anything from you today," the servants shook their heads when he came.

"Then the miller must have made a mistake," the coach man responded. "But you should be able to use this anyway," and he swung the bag across his shoulders and placed it on the ground before the servants.

"It seems to me," Angelica laughed, "that it wasn't the miller who made a mistake, but you. You can't think, can you, that it would be possible to buy me with a simple bag of flour?"

"Of course, that's not what I think," Layosh admitted. "But it was the only way I could see you again. Your beauty has so captivated me that I would give the roof over my head just to see you once more."

106

"Well, if what you say is true, then do it," the beauty stared imperiously into his eyes. "Nobody has ever sold a house because of me and nobody has ever offered me greater proof of their love."

The young coachman bit on his lower lip until it nearly bled, but he could not resist her provocation. The little hut was the only thing he had earned from all his hard work, but his desire for the favor of the enchanting young woman was stronger than his good sense. "Would that really be proof of my love?" he asked. "And if I do it, may I come to you without having to bring you flour?"

"Of course, you may come," Angelica seductively lowered her gaze. "What good man is not allowed to visit an honest house?"

The besotted coach man swung himself back on the driver's seat, but from that day forward he carried no fruit and vegetables to the market in Monastra and no peasants home. He only galloped around, looking for a buyer for his hut. Those who were rich scoffed at what he offered. After all, they could hardly take advantage of his poverty, the poor having no money to steal. Then one evening in the tavern, he happened to meet a broker of sorts who offered him three gold coins for the hut. Despite the low price, Layosh was grateful. He slept in his coach that night and the next day he used the coins to buy a golden chain with an emerald hanging from it.

When he came to see Angelica in her garden, he was the only suitor waiting for her beneath the blossoming apple tree. Layosh's hair was unkempt and his cheeks were gaunt with worry but his eyes gleamed happily and his mouth widened into a smile. He bowed before her and offered his gift.

"Your house must have been worth very little, if you only got for it a thin golden chain and a tiny emerald," said she, but she clasped the necklace around her neck all the same. "Nevertheless, you shall be my guest for breakfast as you must be hungry."

Layosh sat at the richly set table but did not touch the food. His gaze was consumed by the sight of the lovely woman who ate with pleasure, and he was satisfied to drink in her extraordinary beauty. It seemed to him that never before in his life had he been so drunk from love and so immeasurably happy. But then Angelica dabbed the corners of her mouth with a snowy white napkin and unclasped the necklace from her neck. "You mustn't think ill of me," she said. "But emeralds do not suit me the way they should," and she placed the necklace on the table before him. "Pearls are more flattering to my eyes and I really don't know for whom I would be willing to lessen the glory of my appearance."

The besotted coachman looked into her eyes and was soon convinced that pearls were indeed the only decoration equal to her face. He took the emerald necklace and carried it to the market. He quickly found out that he could only get pearls in Sopron. There was nothing left for him to do but to drive his horses forward on the long voyage. He traveled all day and all night. His oldest horse became so weary that Layosh unharnessed him and left him on the side of the road. He sold the remaining three horses along with the coach at the market in Sopron. He got only three gold coins for his last remaining property but he was satisfied that with the coins and the emerald he would have enough to buy a pearl necklace.

He returned on foot to Monastra. He walked for three days and three nights and the soles of his shoes were so worn away by the end of his voyage that all that was left on his feet was dust. And Layosh hadn't even a penny left to buy new shoes. Yet despite his great weariness, he whistled because he was carrying a gift in his breast pocket that would certainly cheer his beloved lady. His tender heart sang and every thought of her gave him the strength needed to complete his journey.

It was early evening when he finally stepped into the court-yard of the white villa at the end of the street. Angelica sat on the veranda lit with torches and passed the time playing cards. "I thought you had forgotten me," she said as if she did not know that a long and difficult journey lay behind him. "But I must confess that your arrival is very welcome to me because my servant is hopeless at cards and I grow dull."

Layosh resisted his overpowering fatigue and reached out for the cards that she dealt to him. The images on the cards danced before his eyes and he could only recall with the greatest difficulty how the game, which he otherwise knew well, was supposed to be played. He didn't want to wait any longer to give her the pearl necklace so he let the game be quickly lost.

"You play even worse than the stupidest of my servants. I can already see that you will be no improvement to my evening," Angelica shook her head scornfully.

"I am tired from my travels," the coachman sighed. "I have been all the way to Sopron and back. Look what I have brought for you." He pulled the string of pearls from his breast pocket and, filled with expectation, laid them down on the table before her.

"When a person is as dreadfully bored as I am, even pearls can do no good," Angelica responded, and she didn't even touch the pearls that lay before her.

"I have traveled day and night. I have sold everything I own to prove to you how I feel about you," Layosh trembled.

"You have indeed proved it to me and I believe you," the haughty beauty smiled as she gathered up the cards. "You must be well satisfied now that this business between us is finished." She stood up and gestured to her servant to accompany him from the house.

"But wait!" the desperate young man cried out. "I now have no roof over my head and no team of horses from which I earned the little I did! And now you just sweep me from your house!"

"I am chasing you out because you claim from me something that I never promised," she was defiant. "I am angry because you believe that you can buy me with a necklace which is not worth as much as the fence around my house."

The coach man was silent. Finally, he wanted to leave.

But when he tried to stand, he found he could not. Because of his long walk, his tired legs had stiffened beneath the table and his back had seized up with a sharp pain. The servants rushed to him and tried to make him stand but they soon concluded that without some honest rest he would not be able to take even one step.

"Make up a bed in the living room and leave him there to sleep," Angelica finally showed some mercy. "But make sure that he is gone before I wake up in the morning. I do not want him to ruin my morning hours with his unbearable pleading."

The servants did as she said and night fell in the white villa at the end of the street. Layosh fell asleep the instant he was laid down. Slumber, of which he had been so desperately in need, dislodged at least for a time the pain pressing against his heart. All the words that the hard-hearted beauty had flung into his face had been true. Yet Layosh could hardly be blamed if his loving eyes had seen things differently than they actually were or if his loving ears heard the words that they desired to hear.

That night Angelica was wakeful. She lay in her bed and tried to fall asleep. Finally, when she could find no peace, she got up and stole into the living room. Layosh lay sleeping on the cot, holding between his fingers the tiny copper vessel that hung from his neck by a leather strap. He pressed it against his cheek and kissed it, murmuring: "My darling mother, you knew what love is, for you loved a Gypsy and because for him you gave up everything else. At least you understand me. And now I finally understand that this is a gift from your heart that you left me and that it is worth immeasurably more than all other riches. Forgive me. I was so blind that tonight I would have given even this to hard-hearted Angelica. But I promise

110

you that I have learned my lesson and I shall never again be so foolish as to place your miraculous gift in the hands of an unworthy woman."

Angelica hid in the doorway and thought long about his passionate words. During all the days that the young coachman had been coming to her garden, she had marveled at the powerful flame of love that burned within him, a flame that no one had ever kindled in her heart. No matter how many ardent and able suitors tried to win her, her heart remained cold and even the most persistent of them finally gave up on her. Now it seemed that the slumbering young man carried in the tiny vessel around his neck a secret potion that might help to thaw her heart. She waited until he was fast asleep and the vessel had dropped from between his fingers. She tiptoed into the living room. She snipped the leather strap with a pair of scissors and carefully slid off the precious vessel.

Her servants accompanied Layosh from the house before dawn. He left the place where malicious voices were already starting to repeat the tale of his unhappy love. He was never seen in Monastra again.

Angelica secretly opened the copper vessel the following morning. In the vessel were a few drops of golden-yellow fluid that smelled of walnut shells and was only cheap perfume to be had in the markets around Budapest. "What foolishness!" the young lady grumbled. "What else could the bride of a Gypsy leave to her poor son but some sour old perfume?" And she pushed it away. A few drops fell on to her finger and Angelica carried the liquid to her face out of feminine habit. The drops burnt so hot and long that she held her palms to her face for some time. When it was still burning, she lifted her face to the mirror and cried out in horror. Her smooth skin had suddenly become all wrinkled. That morning, beautiful Angelica became an old crone.

She washed and scrubbed and rubbed her face but nothing worked. She visited all the best doctors from Budapest to Vienna but none could help her. She squandered all her money for creams and ointments and even sold the white villa at the end of the street but her face remained wrinkled. She was so poor and ugly that people shunned her on the street and children turned away in fright. But no one in Monastra really pitied her. They were convinced that this was the punishment she deserved for her pride and arrogance.

REBECCA AND THE GYPSY

It all happened a long time ago when the roads between the Raba and Mura Rivers were dusty in the summer, muddy in the autumn and barely passable in the winter. Feudal lords traveled along these roads on horses, peasants covered them with teams of oxen and beggars made their way on foot. But no matter how they traveled along these roads, all who did so used to encounter Gusti, the Gypsy fiddler, and Rebecca, the dancer. For the two, having no other home, were always on the roads. Rebecca and the Gypsy traveled from crossroad to crossroad, from village to village, from town to town, and wherever they went, they brought happiness. They stopped in market squares or anywhere at all where people would pause and watch them. But even when they danced and played in the middle of no-where, even when they were watched only by the animals in the fields, they danced and played with all their hearts. Anyone who had once seen and heard them only longed to repeat that pleasure again and again.

People loved the sound of Gusti's fiddle but they were even more enchanted by Rebecca's light-footed dance. When she gave herself to the music, she was no longer of this world. Her bare feet hopped about like a rabbit in the dewy grass, her body undulated like a willow in a spring breeze and her face shone like the morning sun on the low plains. She was young and beautiful as no other and her heartfelt laughter was contagious. When workers in the fields heard the sound of her laughter, they lay down their hoes. In the taverns, even the hungriest patrons forgot where to put their spoons. When they heard that lovely sound, it seemed that time stood still for an instant, that something beautiful stole into their hearts and spread comfort and warmth.

And so it happened one spring day that the young king of Blatograd traveled to the Raba River to fish for trout. His luxurious coach stopped at a corner where a crowd of people had gathered. They stood in a great circle watching a fiddler and a dancer who entertained them with great skill. The king's retinue were pulled in by their curiosity and when the king himself heard the tinkling sound of Rebecca's laughter, he himself tarried for a while among the people. Enchanted, he gazed at her slender body and the sparks that flew from her dark eyes kindled a fire in his heart. Without realizing what he was doing, he drew in closer and closer until he was touching the spinning fabric of her dress and then he grabbed her by the hand.

"I have never seen anything more beautiful than your dance," said the young king when Gusti put down his fiddle. "I have never heard anything more delightful than your laughter," he held Rebecca's hand. She stood still in surprise. "First, I promise before all these good people that I am a man who never goes back on his word, and then, my lady, I offer you my royal hand in marriage."

"Your majesty," answered Rebecca and she kissed his royal hand, "I have never been so honored or so moved. But, sadly, I cannot except your hand because my heart belongs to another: to Gusti, the Gypsy fiddler. And it is only because of our great love that we are able to give so much happiness and joy to others."

"You are far too beautiful and precious to belong to a traveling fiddler," the young king smiled. "I am the only one in all the land who is able to offer you a home worthy of your beauty and charm," he said with conviction. "You shall have everything you ever desired in my court. All of my servants will be at your beck and call."

"But your majesty, I want nothing more than the wind from the plains blowing though my hair and Gusti's hand safely guiding me on these rutted and overgrown paths," Rebecca explained to the young king. "Whenever you desire it, we shall come to your court and cheer you and yours but now I beg of you to leave me with the man I love the most of all," she pleaded.

But the king's command must be respected in the land. His servants carried Rebecca into the gilt carriage and left Gusti alone on the dusty road. The Gypsy fiddler went from crossroad to crossroad, from village to village, from town to town. He went to all the places he had traveled over the years but his song was now sad. He sang of his bottomless pain and it entered the hearts of his listeners and caused tears to come to their eyes. But they could not help him.

The years passed.

Rebecca was rubbed with aromatic oils, dressed in silks and crowned as the queen. Seven maidservants cared for her day and night and seven footmen were always at her service. Each morning, the young king gave her the best food and drink from distant lands. The best musicians in the land played reveilles in the morning and the best dancers tried to lighten her evenings. But Rebecca only closed her eyes. During all the long years she lived at the royal court, she had never once laughed. The king, who loved her with all his heart and had tried in every way to cheer her, also grew sad. A great sadness took up residence in Blatograd. Old people who were one hundred years old could not remember such a time of sadness and their long-dead ancestors had never told them of such a time.

Then one Sunday, the king and queen went to a cow fair. By coincidence, the fiddler Gusti, who trod the whole country with his sadness, was traveling on the same road. When Rebecca heard from afar the sound of his violin, she immediately recognized its voice. She stepped out of her golden shoes, ran among the people and began to dance in the middle of the square as if she were being carried by a whirling wind. Her happy laughter floated through the air and merchants forgot about their customers and let the money fall from their pockets. The king, who saw and heard all of this, felt a pain in his heart and an idea came into his mind. He whispered to his servant, telling him to take care that the traveling musician did not leave the town. Then he returned with the queen to his court.

That night, the king secretly made his way to Gusti who was sleeping in the barn behind the coachman's tavern. He begged him to exchange clothes with him for one day. He wanted to dress up as the traveling fiddler in hopes of cheering up his queen, of luring on to her lips the smile he so desired. Despite the weight of his sadness, Gusti had a good heart and he pitied the unhappy king. He accepted his proposition. He took off his shabby worn-out rags and was soon dressed in the king's splendid clothes. The king put on Gusti's rags and hung Gusti's fiddle over his shoulder.

The guards at the castle allowed Gusti, who looked well in royal garments, to enter the court and after so many years of loneliness, he spent the night at his beloved Rebecca's side. The next morning, a traveling fiddler appeared at the castle gates, but he was not recognized as the king and so was driven away. In this way, Gusti became the king. The smile returned to Rebecca's face and nobody could tear their eyes away from its splendor. The king wandered for the rest of his days from crossroad to crossroad, from village to village, from town to town. He told of his strange fate but nobody believed him.

Translated by Erica Johnson Debeljak

Vinko Möderndorfer

Vinko Möderndorfer *is a director, playwright, poet and writer. He was born in 1958 and graduated in theatre direction from the Academy for Theatre, Radio, Film and Television (AGRFT) in Ljubljana. In the past 25 years he has directed more than 100 theatre and opera performances. His film Suburbs opened the 61st Venice Film Festival and the 28th World Film Festival in Montreal on the same day. Vinko Möderndorfer writes plays, poems (also for children), short stories, novels, TV and film scripts, radio plays for children and adults. He has received several awards, among them the Borštnik Award for best director (1986), the Župančič Award of the City of Ljubljana (1994) for the collection of short stories Krog male smrti (The Circle of Small Death), the Prešeren Fund award for the short story collection Nekatere ljubezni (Some Loves), and many others.*

A SHARED MEMORY

Vinko Möderndorfer

I was standing under a tree. It was a hot summer day. I remember the peace levitating in the air. Perhaps there were also cicadas, birdsong, wind in treetops … I don't know how I got to that tree. I no longer know where the tree was. The tree with a large top. Sometimes I seem to think that there were dry pine needles lying all over under the tree, at other times I recall fruit hanging from its branches. Apples? Pears? I don't know … But I clearly remember the image of the jagged line of pines dividing the earth and the sky on the horizon, and the unpleasant feeling of fear that *I'd been forgotten, alone, that there was nobody I knew in that landscape with the jagged line of the horizon …*

I was a child. Four, perhaps five years old. Too young to remember whether the image of the landscape and the tree above me was a real memory or just a story I'd been told … I may even have dreamt it. The image of the large treetop and the child beneath it might be just part of some dream movie. Perhaps I borrowed the image from somebody else's memories … I might have read about it in some thick book … I don't know … Images, after all, can get mixed up … But … the feeling of vastness and infinity, which inhabited me in early childhood for

119

the first time, is so strong that sometimes I'm certain that the jagged line of the pines dividing the sky and the landscape is a true memory, and *mine alone.*

The memory of the landscape is accompanied by an event. Again I'm not sure if it truly happened. *Events* exist in our memory like dynamic fragments ... We talk about *events* and describe them, but we say nothing about *feelings* ... The feelings are realisations which *change us* (the realisation that the world is large and we're alone in it), while events we sometimes adopt and talk about them as if they really happened to us. And the event which took place in the valley, where a boy was standing under a large treetop, was this: First there was a sound. Gentle humming coming closer ... A car driving down the road. Raising dust. The car meanders in a strange way. The boy under the tree lowers his eyes from the horizon to the road ... The fear that he's lost and alone in the immense world subsides for an instant ... The air trembles ... The eye follows the car ... *This is no longer just an image. It's the continuation of the image.* At a gentle curve the car skids and tumbles into the ditch. *The sounds of the landscape ebb away ... Follows a deaf silence ... And it lasts. Goes on and on. For what seems like a lifetime.* White smoke is coming from the car. Then the vehicle's ablaze, burning with slow and long hissing flames. People come running from the field. They weren't there before. Before, there was only the landscape and the horizon with the irregular line of the pines cutting through the sky ... Now there are people, something is happening, now the image will turn into a memory. The child is standing under the tree like under a huge, safe umbrella, watching the scene helplessly. The farmers pull a child out of the car, and then a man. The girl is wearing a red skirt. Her black shoe lies in the dust ... The car burns down ... Nobody's dead ... The man who was at the wheel, obviously the girl's father, is running around the car in confusion ... Otherwise

120

everything's fine … The landscape is slowly calming down. The wound in it is healing. The sounds return: birdsong, buzzing of the bees, cicadas in the grass, wind in the trees … Now somebody grabs the boy under the tree by the hand, the treetop is suddenly not so big, so sheltering and safe … *There you are!* says the woman holding the boy's hand. The woman is his mother. And she hugs him. The smell of her skirt is also imprinted on the mind. *We've looked everywhere for you. I thought I'd lost you …* The mother bursts into loud sobs. Here the event ends and memory begins …

I no longer know where all this happened … There are quite a few possible places … The village by the sea where I spent a few days when I was five … But there are no pines there … And the pines in my memory were dense and dark dark green … Perhaps it happened on a day-trip to the mountains … But there are no rocky faces in the memory, just a plain and the jagged line of the pines dividing the sky … Mother told me that I got lost once, but she claims it was in the town, in the market place on a rainy Saturday … And that my fear must have come from there … Perhaps the memory is made up of different parts: the pines came from one event, the tree from the other, the car yet from somewhere else and the girl in a red skirt and the shoe in the dust from who knows where … And my fear, fear of loneliness, the realisation that the world is big and endless and a child is lost in it from somewhere completely different …

Many years later, when the memory of the event in the valley was fading and all that remained was the image of the boy under the tree, as if somebody else was watching it, as if somebody was writing some novel without an end, I met her … She was quite ordinary, and I was quite ordinary. She smelt of summer rain, and it was raining when we met one summer. On the inner side of her thigh, just above the knee, she had a mark the size of a palm … *When I was little, we had an accident. I was burnt when they pulled me out of the car.*

As I was kissing the trace of our ancient common memory left by fire on the young and fragrant body, she said: *There was a tree. And a boy standing under it. That is all I can remember.*

Translated by Lili Potpara

Andrej Morovič

Andrej Morovič, *born in 1960 in Ljubljana, is a writer, film maker, photographer, journalist, founder of the Gromki Theatre and one of the leading figures in the Metelkova autonomous cultural centre in Ljubljana. He has helped to organize and/or participated at numerous international festivals (European Month of Culture 1997 – Ljubljana, Slovenia; Expo 2000 – Hannover, Germany; Bitef – Belgrade, Yugoslavia; La polveriera – Rome, Italy; Kukart – St. Peterburg, Russia; Bienale de Sao Paolo 2002 – Sao Paolo, Brasil). Since 1993 he lives and works mostly in Ljubljana, Slovenia. He has published four collections of short stories and seven novels. His short stories have appeared in numerous anthologies.*

EAST 12th STREET, APARTMENT 10

Andrej Morovič

The pigeons are cooing glass beads. From the narrow straits between two houses they are forced to take off helicopter-style. Sounds like rods whipping air. One floor below, a dwarf hysterically fires rounds of Hispanic allegations, the speed almost peeping from behind the sound barrier. Cardboard walls are merciless; they conceal nothing. Mr. Caballero doggedly emphasizes verbs with his chocolate hand, I warned you! Each time a splintered scream, something womanlike, outruns him. For accompaniment – flying shards. Plates shatter longer than bottles. That one was especially heavy. A scooter jitters over the dissected pavement: Bergman's "Wild Strawberries". An inch of a crack under the front-door. Cyclopean cockroaches march cockily and feast on our provisions. Across the hall lives a man with lard in his eyes. His skull is shaven. On it a large wound. Lice suck on the lymph smear and the blood curdles. He is besieged by less frequent, therefore more vehement attacks. When they overwhelm him, he focuses on whacking the door, the windows, his fiancee, his mother and sometimes the neighbours. Once I tried to interfere. There are better ideas around. Even the dark-clad policemen couldn't tame him. Family affair. Like a cell on Death Row where Hope irrevocably withers. Through the main aorta of the central heating system drip the last meager waters mixed with belching bananas of air. It feels like someone were pissing in my ear. The window behind the fire escape stairs, grated and barred, is sifting the feeble morning light. The boiler in the cellar is already cooking fresh steam. Outside slaves in pin-stripes await the starting shot, the firecrackers of anger crumpled between their grinding teeth. Hot fumes begin to press with all their might. Buttock clenching does not help anymore. Before I am burst asunder, with every limb I possess, with all my grunts of vengeance, I succumb to the stream of the raging brook. I straddle the thighs, I'd like to drench the belly from outside. Excitedly I hiccup half a death mantra. I collapse, not caring where it hits the ground. The shower of the damned.

The Painter at E 12th, #14

Directly above us used to live a Russian painter. Twenty years ago he succeeded in escaping from the Soviet Union. He brought along suitcases packed with fear, as well as thirteen employees of the ubiquitous KGB, who trailed behind him like wolfhounds until his death. He lived the lonely life of a God-inspired artist. He seldom left the house. At times he set out on the long voyage to Coney Island, where Russian Jews had their enclave and some ladies appreciated his work. Sometimes they even visited him. On one such occasion, the cold eye of a camera froze him stripped to his waist, showing his bony, strangely beautiful chest. A corpulent aunt with an innocent smile, around her neck a string of pearls, is holding her palm motherly on his frivolous mane of ashen hair. Half seriously, half humorously, the artist is gazing into the greyish-white

126

painting of a bull, mounting a spread-eagled woman's body lying on the floor. No faces. The painting is dominated by the bull's rear, his swinging tail, enormous balls and by oddly straddling hind legs which, in an extraordinarily elongated perspective, conjure up the dynamics of blustering passions. Here and there the ladies persuaded the painter to sell them one of his works of bestiality. He had no other income. His trips drained with the passing of time. The ladies have also become more frail. New York, this cold, metal structure without a hint of meat, had been gnawing up his brittle core with the persistence of a mechanical rat. The KGB systematically increased the pressure, even tapped his REM. Life had, so to speak, become a problem. With steady, resigned patience he stuffed the pores of the fated shell of his loneliness. And when he ran out of pores, Vassily Sitnikow set his blessed soul free. No one noticed the anonymous death. Only the heavenly stink, from day to day more unbearable, forced the neighbours to alarm the police. The firemen in gas masks had to drill a hole into a wall to penetrate the apartment. It was literally packed to the ceiling. And there, in one of the corners, were remnants of a decaying body. In the interest of public hygiene, employees of the Sanitation Department, wavering between indifference and disgust, uncovered layer after layer the fossil imprints of a heart's beat. It was revealed that over the years, the man had crammed the once fussily tidy flat with rubbish galore. He had one of those illnesses, caused by either wars or extreme poverty, where the patient becomes so obsessively frugal that he dare not even breathe out. Like a diligent field mouse in autumn, the painter hoarded and hoarded, initially somewhat valuable things and later anything, indiscriminately. Along with this, order grew into chaos. When there was so much trash that he could no longer open the toilet door he started to squeeze his number two into plastic bags. These he stored all

127

over the place. What he did with his number one, we will never know. The excavation took two weeks. The junk filled up nine large containers. Unbelievable that the floor didn't cave in, the house being so shoddy and shabby. Due to the danger of contamination, the Authorities were careful to prevent looting of the mortal's belongings. These journeyed via hydraulic compactor into the guts of one of the haulers which continously drop garbage blocks onto the bottom of the Atlantic.

The House on Christopher Street

You unlock the gate to the house on Christopher Street No. 85. With pride, since few are the fortunate who get to live here. In the portal of love, in the anus of the West. The latch clicks sickly behind you and you take off the coat of haughtiness, for inside the truth is different.

The dwelling A1 is empty, guarded by sharp vapours of fresh paint. Somebody passed away. The rent jumped from three to fifteen hundred dollars. A replacement will be found, that's for sure.

For decades A2 has been occupied by a lady of German origin. Every summer she is choked by the foulness of the decaying rubbish which blooms at the end of the narrow courtyard. It is overlooked by the only window that A2 possesses. She closed, sealed, glued and barricaded it. She defends herself with joss sticks and rose water, with mirrors, lavender curtains, ruffles and chiffon. Instead of the sun, a violet lamp flares. Chests, lace doilies, plastic flowers. Pictures, photos, peep holes into the past. As if all is wrapped with a cyclamen gauze. This is Sartre's fleshy, pale pink and willing Marcelle. This will be Ajar's madame Rosa.

An invisible man squats in A3. He has a large dog and had a small one. He copulates regularly with the big one, so the general opinion goes. Recently, for whatever reason, he mounted the little one. Desperate whining accompanied a tearing of the ass. Presumably it didn't work. The man lost his nerve, strangled the mongrel and destroyed the family idyl. All has been quiet since then. Mourning in the house. The lovers fondle carefully, so as not to offend the deceased. The loneliness doubled.

Reggae and the odour of good grass emanate day and night from the cavern next door. At odd times it swallows or spits out a quartet of gauzed faces.

A5 and A6 are rented to respectable citizens, identified by the exact trotting of the soles and penetrating smell of clean clothes and Elle perfume.

A7 is Arthur, the piano player in the Indian summer of life, gay, exquisite manners, very extravagant. From here on, gas masks are obligatory. The unpleasant stench, which on the ground floor merely pinched the nostrils, becomes unbearable; it almost wrenches the nose off your face. You'd run if the heat hadn't already sucked out the last milliamperes of strength.

You pass another lonely man with a German sheppard. Two best friends, for a change. Now speeding past Amparo from Puerto Rico, an astute evaluator of us people. By 13, a den of two weakened old women, venting the suffocating reek. They scold each other constantly, complicate their life, and thus gnaw on. Yet another day. Yet another victory. The door is usually kept wide open. The food fossils in burnt pans are creeping, the worms are restless, looby-looing on the teflon. The old women watch the corridor, always greeting extremely amiably. You return a smile of pure sympathy, trying to supress the urge to vomit. Your Lover's apartment definitely seems like a paradise when you are finally rescued, dashing to the window, ajar. The street is still swarming. The fire escape is luxuriously spacious, a convenient location for a real Sunday picnic. Pity it's dangerously corroded by rust. Coming to your senses again, you plant a fleeting kiss on Lover's ear lobe. Everything is somewhat crooked – low ceiling, rotting floor, drunk walls and furniture. You lift the cover of transparent plastic into which real pennies, dimes, quarters and even a dollar bill are sealed. You sit down so it won't spray, and piss with relief. The hairs on your balls dance like the tendrils of an irate octopus. You step to the sink. Softly you feel around her waist, bosom, you charm the neck with a cooling breath and gentle lip crawl. The collar-bone twitches, the shoulders rise, the head tilts to your side. Her hair flutters over your ears and face. The moment of love turns towards you, embraces you like morning sun rays do a numb reptile, presses onto you, quivering. You kiss. You lick where it's sweet, salty, sour, you stretch all the way to the bitter. A visit to saliva geysers, across the gums and dwellings of assorted germs. You glide towards uvula, touch the palate. It's palatable. The mattress sighs discreetly. With chessman's patience, you repeat the process of rediscovering each other's bodies. You dive into yourselves, like grebes after fish. Underneath your bed dwarfy mice go about their daily tasks. They gorge, shit, multiply and watch TV. Steel wool puffs in their holes don't interfere with their *joie de vivre*. Same with glue traps. Through the ceiling penetrates the cough of an older leftist film maker, her hair like a sea sponge. The rumour goes that she never washes it. She lives amidst inpenetrable heaps of old Village Voices and similar magazines. She is determined to catch the nauseating Establishment in a lie. So revealingly that it will forever sink into a grave of shame. Lover is now completely yours. You rummage through her most secret pockets. Lucky you. Along the edge of a sill, above your heads, cockroaches defiantly march by. In devotion, you cover her eyes so she doesn't have to watch. You swallow stringy spittle. You try to concentrate, to belong to this one, the only one. Amparo is angry, she fusses

130

loudly. She says you have a bad temper. The neighbours are also having sex, if your ears don't deceive you. They're so normal, it's obscene. The film maker detests men. Nothing more understandable in this world. Her neighbour is her own daughter. Slender as the Flatiron Building. Various lovers are passing the baton. The apple falls far, far from the tree. Ends up in a glass bottle, with preservatives without a name. You too swallow her furtively with your eyes. You'd stick the knotty elongation wherever you could. You'd like to feel something. Some prickly warmth inside, a proof that there is something in you. That something is happening. Caution, ejaculation.

Through the steamy smog, the summer is hammering the flat roof, melting the rug of tar cardboard. Still as a praying mantis, but not as green, you lie on a towel, on top of carefully spread-out newspaper sheets. It's too far to the ocean. Greasy sweat dribbles down your butt gorge. Soaks one of the standard speeches of President Georgie B. Your Lover is roasting only a foot away. Exposing the pelvis, the loins and the white skin above her private property. Sucks in the burning electrons. A human battery. Already full. Spilling over. The satin cleft emits familiar aromas. You are well hidden. In American freedom, this is how you're allowed to be a nudist. You don't touch, since the towel can shift and get soiled forever. Lover may as well be dead. You too. You can't resist the assault of the rays. You peep over the roof top. Moving matter bustles about in the blurred cauldron. An olive house rests on the corner of Bleeker and Christopher. During the Gay Pride Day parade, when hundreds of thousands were flowing by, there was a naked posterior hanging out of every window. A rainbow of saturated peaches. A trace of relaxing wit in a slightly different day.

You sleep as if on toothpicks. The noise from outside launches you to the window. Three toxic fellas are beating up a middle-aged black man. A popular sport for the guys from across the river. Drudgery of work throughout the week, crusades into the Mecca of entertainment at the weekend. Violence extends beyond disbelief. The day is breaking out vehemently. The most deprived jobholders are rushing to trade in their life juice for readies. They turn around for a second and keep on hurrying. How tiny they all are! You're too cut off to call anybody. What was that number anyway? The old women across the hall surely are fast asleep. Their rubbish dances a slow tango. Without any panic the insects whirl to life, hoard riches, devise the future. Small creatures with their feet firmly on the ground. The more intellectual castes feed on you; thoughtfully digesting Genet, they are pricking you lazily now and then. The plagued air triggers your asthma. Your sweetheart who sometime, somewhere, was treasuring your love, has oozed away like jelly. You try to keep her together, not to lose her through your fingers. You try to protect her, not knowing from what. What happened? In your lungs squats sorrow, bitterness, guilt, in your heart ruthlessness, in your liver anger, in your kidneys fear, in your spleen worry, between your balls and anus insecurity. Soon the alarm clock will croak. You'll have to get up, give your blood submissively, to prolong your apathy with bread, water and shelter.

Christopher Street Stop

The chrome-silver subway races at full speed. Tossed back and forth, it looks like a bleeding "Kinshu-Snake of Horror" from some cheap Japanese SF thriller. Last tremors. The express train dashes by the local station and fills it to the hilt with a murderous noise. Condensed moisture trickles down, persistently peeling old ceramic tiles off the concrete walls. Coldness and stale stench shift places according to a complex protocol.

The platform is almost empty; every megalopolis has its time-out. A homeless person lies on a bench. His head, cracked at the neck, hangs limply across the hand support. What he wears is his kingdom. The narrator is hunched in the opposite corner. Slightly delirious from a splitting hangover and lack of sleep, he watches distrustfully the stillness of the filthy soles. Perky clouds of museum ripe body odours swirl around his nostrils. Stage left an extra in a grotty overcoat approaches them, unobtrusively pulls his hand out of his pocket and swiftly evolves into the main character by lunging for the man's formidable erection, his morning stick. The witness stares agog at this horror; his rubber limbs hamper a hasty retreat. The raincoat shuffles away – nothing happened, right? Very quickly he comes back however, cannot resist, he grabs again, already more courageously, and sighs excitedly: Wow, it's... big! Bigger still is his delight. The moral imperative or perhaps just a myopic gaze straight into the blind spot, mercilessly washes him away from the cherished object. Not for long though. He keeps returning to his beloved site. He caresses the protruding member with increasing eagerness. Meticulously, like a systematic gourmet he examines the strength of the smooth muscle. With a flat hand he rubs it down and up, reverently looking at the spectator. He's leering at you! With a good-natured, almost gentle smile on his lips he murmurs: It's really big, this giant black ferule. All the while never granting the sleeping man a single Band-aid from his gleaming pupils.

Under my Window

During the heat wave, when everybody's cerebral tripe begins to simmer, the avenue is lively without respite. Metal caterpillars and worms trundle in the middle, framed by people milling, loitering or hustling along the sides. Seated, some spectate the

133

unfurling of the non-events. With arms on their knees, heads hanging slackly, their legs jitter in time with the rattle of ghetto blasters. Ay, ay, Milonga! Under the Dominican shops' garish plastic awnings, clumps of frisky figures crowd the faint shade. Popular activities include drinking, shouting, shoving and sending smoke signals. Whining children break free from irritated grasps, mothers hot in pursuit.

The small vegetable shops exhale unleaded odors of rotting fruit and sweating banknotes. The Chinese speedy-food restaurant blasts miasmic cannonades of posthumous chickens which have never seen the sun - cantata for the conveyor belt and greasy lips. Sitting on the fire escape, there's hardly room for one, I sip dark beer. Right beneath me the house dealer consciensciously mans the entrance door step. When I was still a novice he consistently pestered me, now we barely acknowledge one another. Bald heads and baseball caps dart around him, erforming passages of a complex score of concrete music. I am extra careful where I flick my ash, anxious to avoid unnecessary trouble.

The music, traffic noise and disharmonious crowing of vocal chords rise and fall in a perpetual chain until evening, when the elderly pack up their infants and withdraw. The cast changes in a slow dissolve. I, too, retire. Time to watch the evening news.

A charlatan mother with a genuine baby and pram moves into the frame. At intervals uncles appear, caress the baby goochy-goochy-goo and reach under its head, where small plastic vials are nesting, half full with yellowish clods of crack. Behind the infant's tiny ears, lo and behold!, there grows a mound of banknotes. Sporadically the mother worryingly bends down to deposit them into her bra. Then she drags her feet into the grocery store across the street, leaving the sucker in front of the door. I see how she furtively exchanges some niceties inside, passes on the relatives' greetings or somesuch, returns in a few moments, treads down the accelerator and storms towards new pastures. Through the grating (our defense against burglars which cost us three thousand dollars), through the fly screen, solidly hidden behind an ochre curtain, I scrutinize a life which I dare taste only in milligrams.

If I tilt my head towards the mirror mounted for this sole purpose, my sight extends all the way to the corner of Columbus and the disreputable 104th, where nervous youngsters patrol in threesomes. Those I'm afraid of, since they've reached the advanced stage of their crack lessons. Any of them would insert a blade under the lobe of your lungs for the smallest of trifles. They just carry a few vials in their pockets, so there's not much damage done in throwing them away if need be. The rest of them faithfully wait in handy caches. I know where almost all these lairs of evil are. To be honest, this is no art, since on the avenue nobody pretends much, except for us, the unparticipating ones, who diligently look the other way. The hiding places are simple and usually shifted frequently; alas the cars of a radio-taxi enterprise always seem to be in vogue. I once stepped into the head office, conveniently located across the street, to inquire how much a day trip to Magic Mountain would cost. To my discomfort I caught the last part of a swift whisper, a piercing glare and a rude:

"What do you want?"

Since then, I secretly think that people transportation is a rather secondary affair to them. Parked by the edge of the catwalk there is, especially at night, a large number of fairly dented sedans, with or without chauffeurs. The vials cringe behind the bumpers, hibernate in the exhaust pipes and lurk between the radiator grills.

Two, maybe three hours past midnight business activities die down. The small, 24-hours-a-day stores attract the last exhausted moths. This is the time I put on my tattered zebra-striped trousers, pull on my parachuter's boots, slide into my thirty-year-old pilot's jacket and, chemical mace firmly in my fist, slip out. Everything is defined and wired to the extent that a person not belonging there, in spite of the appearance to the

135

contrary, is almost not endangered. You're an outsider, so you don't exist. I like that. To smell The Land of Dung, just before a new day splatters it with a fresh layer of colour. I don't venture too far though, only to the store next-door to buy some more beer. This gives my presence an excuse. The conversation breaks off the moment I enter. Small gentlemen with Bud cans in their hands stare at me with vacant, I assume hostile, eyes. Since the vendor remains impassive I'm allowed to leave.

Perhaps around four, when everything becomes relatively quiet and even the rattle-traps clatter a little more sleepily, I will go to bed.

Every so often some inhuman screaming spurs me up to the window, denuded peepers bulging in anticipation of a bloody polka, yet forevermore remaining disappointed. Usually, two gangs, each on its side of the avenue, fling bottles and/or bricks at each other. Just kidding.

Early in the morning, the monstrous noise of rubbish trucks annihilates me. Right under my window, located at the top of a slight incline, they run their growling engines and compress the trash. They are in mafia's hands down to the last one, dark green, decorated with kitschy yellow inscriptions, clearly reflecting Moorish influence.

When I first moved into this charming kennel, encouraged by the gridiron, I pushed up the window and with superhuman strength hollered:

"Go fart somewhere else," adding:

"Fuck you, you fuck!" – a pleasantry I learned one day while trying to single out a halfway edible apple from a heap of putrefying Grannies.

The rumble was so loud, I didn't even cause ridicule.

Only later did I consider what those machete swinging savages could have done to me.

Translated by Gerald Hansen and the author

Maja Novak

Maja Novak, born 1960 in Jesenice, Slovenia, graduated from the Faculty of Law in Ljubljana. Unable to find employment in the legal profession, she began to work as a self-employed translator and writer. In 1990 she spent a year as a secretary and translator on a building site in Mafraq, Jordan, and later worked as a journalist. She has published ten books for grown-ups and children, and translated about forty. She was nominated for several important literary awards and received the Prešeren Fund prize in 1997. She translates from English, Italian, French and Serbian. In 1999, her novel *Beyond the Congress* was published in Finnish. Her short stories have been included in a number of anthologies.

THE TOMCAT

Maja Novak

Even as a little girl I had a clear notion that a grown-up, mature person could only have one goal in life: to be reincarnated after death as a tomcat.

Yet many are called, but few are chosen. That is good. After all, not all of us can be tomcats; what on earth would we eat if there were no cows and no pigs? And no fish, but those I don't count. The ones in my cans are dead. Very much so. Dead for a long, long time.

Therefore it doesn't suffice to know what pays when one is good and quiet but one also needs to make a little effort. Just a tiny one, mind you. Therein lay the mistake which hindered my transformation into a tomcat for quite a few years. It was not the lack of trying. I tried; indeed, I tried too hard. Healthy cats sleep soundly at least sixteen hours a day. Scientists have not as yet discovered to what they owe this enviable ability. When a tomcat is awake, he whiles away this time napping; I, though, was a hyperactive child; so very hyperactive, in fact, that my first encounter with the outside world was simultaneously an encounter with authorities.

A policeman demanded to know who the hell tied a beer bottle to the tail of a service dog. "In broad daylight!" complained my mother later on, "And in the middle of the road!" "And on a Labrador, too!" further defined the whereabouts of the bottle my father, speaking with an admiration he was unable to conceal no matter how hard he tried.

The Labrador stuck in my memory since the story was all about me and the naming of the dog only gave it additional charm. Otherwise, up to this day I'm unable to tell the difference between a greyhound and a German shepherd. A dog is a dog. The policeman's dog was first and foremost a dog in my eyes – as soon as I saw it I knew I loathed it deeply. It smelled different from a cat and that is all one needs to know.

While the parents of other three-year-olds were losing their nerve because their kids were madly afraid of dogs, my father and mother were losing theirs because I wouldn't even as much as consider fearing them.

The anxiety of my folks was such that I was infected by it as well. Whenever with my mom's nail-clippers I'd transformed a pure-breed's tail into a tricoloured cocarde, I was afterwards deeply distressed. I kept asking myself why I dared to get close to the mutts while my buddies were expected to run away screaming right under the wheels of a truck; and I shuddered at the thought that I was not normal.

Until I met Donovan.

Donovan was a Persian cat of an aunt of my father's who inherited us after her death. He was the same colour as my best white mohair sweater after I'd (not quite accidentally) smeared it with apricot ice cream, and as hairy as my sweater had been before I creatively altered its appearance.

Are you getting the impression I'm heaping up pronouns? I love pronouns. Me. My. Mine. Meow.

Donovan was a normal enough cat. For a regular cat, possesion is something enduring. After he buys or inherits or is given custody of his people or wins them in gambling – or perhaps they are given to him as a present – he acknowledges them with a crocodile yawn and then forgets all about them. Later on, he takes them off the shelf only when he needs them; beyond that, he doesn't waste his time with them. It is important to keep in mind that a cat is awake only eight hours a day and that he mainly spends this time napping. And his memory is not brilliant. Therefore he is, day by day, forced to do in those scanty few hours everything that the majority of us won't experience in all of the statistically adjudged seventy-eight years of our life. Can you imagine a cat saying: "I won't make love today since I've already done it last year and therefore know how it's done?" Certainly not. A cat is born anew every morning and is delighted about it. Experiences need to be relived again and again, whereas people are fixed stars on a cat's horizon (they read each book only once and tend to tolerate the same child for about twenty years), therefore they are considered to be boring.

Donovan walked through people.

Not close to them but literally through them. I didn't believe it until I saw it with my own eyes. And then no one believed me. I realized only later that the reason I was able to see it was because I, likewise, was born to be a tomcat. Here is what happened. My mother was walking through our house with a comb and a brush in her hand. "Donnie, Donnie!" she was calling, wanting to comb him. Donovan was approaching her in the same straight line she was moving along. But he was not thinking about her or about the combing. He was thinking about a sparrow perched outside on a forsythia branch, and was anxious to find out what a sparrow with no head would look like. Donovan was so preoccupied with his thoughts that he stepped right through my mother's leg (not between her legs, which would be quite unremarkable) – he stepped through her body as if she weren't there. As if, assisted by some sorcery, he transported himself to the other side of her swollen

141

leg, swaddled for her varicose veins. And no one but I noticed anything. Donovan didn't notice anything because he was lost in his thoughts, and my mother didn't notice anything because she was a mere human, therefore hopelessly dumb.

But after I saw Donovan with my mom I also saw Donovan with a dog.

Donovan was a pleasure to behold. He weighted eleven kilos. His grumpy face hung under his nape which was sinewy and muscular like a bull's. When he was in his amorous state, the whole house smelled of an expensive French perfume, slightly warmed up. If he chose to hit a closed door with his big haunches, he'd open it by sheer impact. But of course he would never consider doing such a thing. Instead, whenever he found himself facing a door that was only slightly ajar instead of respectfully waiting for him wide open, he sat and waited quietly for someone to come by and push it open enough for his meter long silky whiskers to pass through unimpeded. He was not fussing. He never complained. He was never offended. He just sat and waited, patiently. The last time I saw him he'd been sitting and waiting for four hours. After I'd pushed the door open he sprung up and walked through as if in a hurry.

But in spite of Donovan's virility it remains an indisputable fact that the dog we're speaking about was at least four times bigger than him. Donovan was striding down our street deep in thought. He paused a few times, licking his upper lip, pleased with himself: the street smelled of him, therefore it was, by international law, his domain. On it, however, the dog had the audacity to appear. Donovan blocked his way. The dog snarled: how dare you, little twerp, tell me where to walk? And he lowered his head.

People said that meant attack. Contrary to their belief, the dog and Donovan knew exactly what it was all about. It was high drama, a display of mocking: shall I lower my head, o tiny

142

one, to see you better? Donovan dropped into a crouch. Glued to the asphalt there was a vertical projection of a cat about half a meter in lenght, half a meter in width and one millimeter high. Donovan crouched and waited to see what the canine idiot would do next. The canine idiot allowed himself one joke too many and, like all authors of insipid jokes, accompanied it with roaring laughter.

How pathetic! How utterly immoderate! We, tomcats, are just discussing whether that crazy Spanish cat who had one ear missing because he got mixed up in territorial disputes between local cats and a barbarous stray, had anything else on his mind but his sweetheart's eyes when he wrote "green, I love you green" ...

Am I getting entangled? For God's sake, we, tomcats, don't chase mice in straight lines! What I'm trying to say is that our breed is at least *discussing* why literary statements about green eyes *function* even if they do seem trite; whereas the dogs still consider it the best entertainment to hit another dog on his butt with a leather belt because he's climbed a mountain he'd never climbed before ... Unbelievable. As if not all places were the same. Either they smell of you or they don't. That is all one needs to know.

At any rate, the dog laughed at Donovan, and people, gathering around to watch (my mother's sweaty hand hysterically clutching mine), said that he snarled. Donovan inched forward without actually moving a muscle and hissed like a snake. They said the dog barked. In truth he was uttering something that would, if translated from animal into human language, sound approximately like: "Suck your prick, you fucking motherfucker!" Which, in spite of an obvious pleonasm, can be considered quite smart, coming from a dog. Donovan took a step backwards. People said it meant surrender. But in truth he gave a speech – a heroic speech that went like this: "Achilles' cursed anger

143

sing, o goddess, that son of Peleus, which started a myriad sufferings for the Achaeans." Such speeches surely sound better when delivered from a certain distance.

The dog said, quoting Milosevic: "I can't hear you!", and he bared his teeth.

People said: "He's going to kill him!" By this, most meant the dog, but a few enlightened ones (not including my mother) meant the cat.

Donovan unglued himself from the ground and, as if by magic, changed dimensions. What used to be a projection of a tomcat measuring half a meter by half a meter by one millimeter, became an arrow, reaching from here to eternity. The dog's muzzle gaped. From surprise. "He's going to do him in!" screamed enthusiastically the audience, which consisted of ninety percent humans and five cats. The cats were sharpening their claws in utter boredom, since the dog and Donovan were not a part of their story.

The cat flew through bared, dripping dog's jaws (the maneuver familiar to us from the story about my mother's legs) and landed in the dog's eye. The dog was left with one, and Donovan with a smudge on his silver-blue claws. In an instant the number of dogs on Donovan's street decreased considerably. Before, there used to be one smirking dog (or barking, depending on your point of view), and then there were none. The dog that was no longer, wailed heartbreakingly.

My father, from whom I've inherited my true understanding of karma and reincarnation, said admiringly: "Jeeesus!" My mother attempted to drag me away. My father tried to pat Donovan.

Donovan looked at him scornfully: "Why dost thou disturb me, o unworthy human, in my moment of hero's sad and bitter victory?"

Pa retracted his hands, bowing slightly.

Donovan looked at his claws and gave the signal of disgust measuring five on his seismological scale.

Donovan's seismological scale applies to measurements of the quality of cat food, but is used occasionally to express deeper feelings and moral judgements about the world he condescends to dwell in.

Four paws, deliberately shaken one after another, signify the highest level of alert, but can translate quite easily into human language. The signal simply means: yes, it's true that I've caught this myself but it does not even cross my mind that I should actually eat it.

And after I'd seen Donovan disposing of the dog with one swipe of paw, I ceased being ashamed of the fact that I was not afraid of them. Some of us simply aren't and my father approves and says: "Jeeesus!" Thus he's lovingly addresing Donovan who is a tomcat. But I, also, am not afraid of dogs. When I'm not afraid of dogs, my mother bursts into tears, saying to my father: "She's just like your aunt who's left us this damned cat and whose own fault it was that she died; what on earth was she thinking, swimming in the cold Bohinj Lake at her time of month!" But my father laughs at my mother and rubs my head as he'd rub Donovan's if the tomcat would let him. Whenever I act like a tomcat my father praises me as he'd praise the tomcat. On the basis of these two premises, major and minor, we can therefore easily deduce the following syllogism: my father loves me because I am a tomcat.

Donovan's revelation had yet another positive aspect: it helped me to overcome my self-consciousness about being short.

The realization that I was smaller than my peers came simultaneously with remembering snatches of conversation whispered in my presence. So emphatically were they whispered as if my parents wanted me especially to commit them to my memory, and they were whispered so often that I had no choice but doing so, although in those days my main interest was in finding out how many paw-swings it took Donovan to wipe a blackbird out of existence.

"Just like your bloody aunt, she is ... One meter forty, when she grew up. No wonder it killed her while she was taking a swim. And at her time of month too! And in the cold, cold Bohinj Lake! Don't tell me that was accidental. The woman was fed up with herself ..."

Says my mother to my father. In a way which leaves it unclear whether she worries about my short legs or relishes the fact that they are the fault of somebody else. E.g. my aunt who'd died almost a year before I was born.

Unusually enough, my father's already home. For they've closed all the pubs on Donovan's street. He's brought his drinking buddies along. That gives him courage. There's strenght in numbers. To one of my mother's there are three of his almost sane drinking pals who admire my father since twenty years ago when he'd to lean my head on while listening to what follows. What follows is beyond my understanding, but when I ask Donovan to clarify he merely shakes his head and says:

"When you grow up, you'll understand."

In the meantime, my father and the rest of Korzak brothers embark on a detailed conversation concerning my body.

"Poison comes in small bottles."

Says one of them, making a gesture as if getting poison inside himself. I am puzzled. If I were to poison myself, I'd stuff arsenic or whatever down my throat, not inside the fly of my pants.

My father is smiling inanely. My mother stares at the thing she would be frying in the pan if it hadn't got burned long ago.

"The most important thing about legs," says a buddy, safely anchored to a glass full of schnaps, "is that they reach to the ground."

"Or up to the ..." adds the next Korzak brother meaningfully, and giggles.

"Or around," says enigmatically the third and, thank God, the last one. His not so crystal clear comment is met with peals of laughter. My mother swings the charred pan as if she intended to throw it at somebody's head. By now, any reasonable cat would have had enough. Not the Korzak brothers, however, who, at a certain point in their lives, had almost graduated from some sort of university.

Next they take up art history. This at least I am able to follow thanks to piles of leather-bound books with reproductions of apparently important paintings, dating from my father's student days. But for some reason I still have the impression that they are talking about me.

"Toulouse-Lautrec," says my father with the voice of a connoisseur.

"And what an artist he was!" says Korzak number two who at least has an idea of who my father is talking about.

147

"All those whores he's painted," adds Korzak number three who has a telepathic agreement with the number two.

"In spite of ..." says my dad, pointing to his trousers which measure about one meter eighty in length and are observed by Donovan with that characteristically curved corner of his black elastic lip. Like a small cynical lion. I deduce that he has no opinion about my father's statement, but it bothers him greatly that the trousers stink.

"He sure shagged a lot of them," comments Korzak number four who has not a clue who Toulouse-Lautrec was, but whose healthy, down-to-earth conclusion is, that whenever art is mentioned it necessarily involves something dirty.

"Oh, yeah," agree the Korzak brothers enviously.

"In spite of ..." says my dad, caressing his trousers complacently.

Donovan leaps up. He buries his front claws into the linoleum and starts walking backwards with his hind legs as far as they go, his front legs not moving. The cat resembles a viaduct. While he's constructing a viaduct, the cat is yawning, blasé.

"Let's go," he says.

"Where to?" I ask, surprised.

He gives me a gentle, pitiful look. "What do you mean, where to? Out. There's night outside. It smells. It's such fun, trying to figure out where the smells come from. If you don't keep your nose close to the fence you are walking on, you'll never find out. And colors are just black, white and blue, and that is so beautiful. Crickets sing but that should not fool you – the little devils are too fast to catch – but if you are really lucky you might run into a big, fat, feisty rat. Its scent on the fence will lead you to it. Believe me – you only need to climb onto the fence and things happen." He licks his upper lip and makes a cut into the linoleum with one swing of his paw, while my mother, seeing it, bursts into tears.

148

"But Donovan," I say with a mixture of excitement and longing, "there is no way I can balance myself on a fence."

He gives me a contemptuous look. "How can you possibly know that," he mews coldly, "if you've never tried?"

In the meantime I kept going to school during the day and was as hyperactive as ever. And since my parents were otherwise at a loss what to do with me, they enrolled me in the lycee and had me decide what to study at the university. With my figure (remember my short legs?) there was no way I could become a forest engineer; other colleges demanded far too much studying which would interfere with my sleeping time considerably – you may recollect I need sixteen hours. Thus the only thing left was anything to do with art.

It was then I remembered someone, sometime, somewhere saying: "Toulouse-Lautrec." Very well, I thought, let it be. I learned to sign my name with red initials in a red circle and drew a portrait of my fat mama in her underwear, the way she would look if anyone in the last eighteen years had a chance to see her in her underwear. Since in all other respects my style was far from original, particular or exceptional, the professors at the art academy, always on the watchout for gifted, authentic young competition, had no problem accepting me. So far, so good.

Except, not everything so good, since my father was taken, owing to Korzak's syndrome, to the mental asylum in Polje and my mother given sole custody, which enabled her to decide about my fate. And she's had her heart set on paralegal school from the very beginning. "With such education," she claimed, "you'll at least be able to support yourself."

There was no mention of me being able to support my children, since there existed an unspoken agreement I'd never have any: I was a grown-up woman and no taller than a meter forty. And when I had my monthly thing I had to conceal it from my mama, for otherwise she'd hide from me the key to the bathroom where a tub with cold water stood. I fought for that key relentlessly since, like any other cat, I liked to be neat and clean. However, I was not that interested in the mirror hanging above the tub, though the image in it was not altogether unattractive – a triangular face with a broad brow and big amber eyes, small chin and a lively mouth – but since mama declared that I was never to have a man, that was that. My mother's views, no matter how foggy because of her spiritual paralysis, were always eventually accepted by me because of my easy-going lethargia.

To make her happy I went to have a look at the paralegal school.

Corridors were narrow, lit with neon light which cats detest, and I had the impression they were saturated with a suspicious smell. I soon figured out why: when I first saw the students I thought I'd wandered into a pack of Doberman, Poodle and Cocker Spaniel bitches. Only after looking closer did I realize they were girls. They wagged their tails, shoved and pushed, crawled over each other and yelped excitedly. Their tongues hung out and they were dribbling each time a male dog came by. One of them was cradling her notes from lectures. Others sniffed greedily as their owner crouched jealously over them, barking furiously at the intruders. It was the time of dog appraisals, called exams. When the judge, also known as professor, called any one of them into his chambers she whined quietly, her sides were heaving as if she was about to get a vaccination shot, and her legs were slipping on the vinyl floor as they dragged her inside by the collar. If she lived through it the rest of them would cram around her, patting her approvingly, screeching with joy and jumping up and down in a most undignified manner.

I went home and told my mother to stick the paralegal school up her you know what, packed my suitcase and declared solemnly I was able to handle the art academy without her help. Donovan didn't have time to say good-bye. With a neighboring tomcat, he was engaged in a life-or-death fight over a scrawny Siamese who in the meantime was gulping food nonchalantly from Donovan's bowl.

At the art academy I met a hairy student who smelled like Donovan and said he liked my courage as well as the fact that I reminded him, in an indefinite way, of Toulouse-Lautrec. Together we rented an attic studio by Ljubljanica river. I didn't love him but I tolerated him willingly, since after spending nights with him I felt less tense than usual and was delighted that I, too, had finally inherited someone.

We were starving.

When you're hungry you feel like crying without being sad (hunger leaves no room for sadness) while simultaneously observing yourself from a distance, as if watching someone else's whimpering and wailing and detesting that person because of it. You hate yourself. You hate everybody in your vicinity. You want to kill all people with full bellies. You'd want to head a revolution, not to change anything but to get a licence to kill. Not with a gun; with a knife; with your bare hands so you'd feel hot sticky blood between your fingers. Yes, you'd kill, but right now are too lethargic to even turn off a transistor radio. The radio drives you out of your mind. You hate it. You hate the voice of the political commentator on the radio because she had breakfast. You detest the starving people of Ethiopia she's talking about because they are just such a stinking, apathetic, sticky heap of messy hair as you are. Naturally, you are unable to paint, for there is not even a grain of truth in the common belief that misery gives birth to the best art. You don't really care that you are unable to paint. You hate paintings and everything beautiful because it is beyond your reach. But even if you were given the best Utrillo, you wouldn't bat an eyelid. You no longer know what you want. There is a lovely view through the window. You hate it and you hate your hungry partner because he dares to mention it.

Pigeons fly by. Pigeons coo on a steep roof.

"Where are you going?" asks my hairy male. Hollowly, disinterestedly, because he's hungry.

Something inside me flutters like a loose sail. The membrane in my nostrils burns and my lips feel as if they were swelling up. Blood pounds in them. I am itching under my fingernails. The outlines of things surrounding me are sharp as a Damascus blade and colours crisply clean like summer nights after rain. All at once I feel a surge of joy and an immense love for my hairy male. I feel power and lust within, lust that a bed cannot quench.

In one jump I reach the edge of a casement window and clasp it with my fingers. I feel tiny, steely muscles in my fingers and it gives me joy that they are so long and so flexible. I pull myself up on my hands, push the shutter open with my shoulders and slither thru the narrow slot like a snake. I climb on the roof. It is orange. I like colour orange. Crouched, I run across the tiles toward the ridge. There is a fat, pearly grey pidgeon in front of me. I press my outstretched arms against the tiles, I arch my back, I glue my stomach and my pelvis to the warm roof. I like warm. My stomach and pelvis are drinking the warmth of the tiles. I curve my feet, curl up my toes. The wind that smells of ozone and jasmine blows from the right direction. The pidgeon has not noticed me. I smell the wind and then, without giving a thought to my movements, I find myself atop of the bird. With all ten fingers I take hold of its swelling chest, I burrow my nails into its soft flesh and bite thru its jugular. Sweet blood spurts out in jerks, drips down my chin onto my blouse and breasts. However, I do not let go of my prey. I lie spread-eagled on the roof, I relax. Then, pleasantly tired, soft and heavy, I slide down to the window and drop right through it, landing on my feet without having to bend my knees. I hold the pidgeon in my teeth. Its wings tickle my neck. The bloody blouse is sticking to my breasts. Food. My hairy male stares. I love him. I have brought him my prey to share it with him. I drop the bird at his feet and sit on my heels. I sit on my heels and I watch him. I want to make love to him. The lower part of my belly pulsates evenly, warmly. The nipples on my breasts are swelling under the red stains on my blouse.

He winces, he averts his eyes, he presses his fist to his mouth, he looks around with unspeakable disgust, lost, as if he'd just waken up from a nightmare, still not knowing where he is. Then he dashes out of the studio as if chased by all the devils of the hell.

Defeated in love, defeated in art (and hungry), I return that autumn, after the birds on my roof are all gone, to Donovan and my mother.

Donovan is blind in one eye. It's as white as an opal and has no depth. The scrawny Siamese is pregnant again although already surrounded by several furry apricot kittens whom she deals with in a neurotic, over-protective manner, like all the Siamese. Donovan doesn't give a damn about his offspring. He is as old as the world itself. He's recently developed the habit of lying atop the fresh laundry that my mother dries on the stove in the winter, and his food must be placed in front of the stove. In Polje asylum, my father hung himself from a doorknob.

I still paint at times.

My work is worthless. And whenever I am forced to confront my own sterile canvases I feel as humiliated as if I were kicked in public. I am no good. What is lacking in my paintings is lacking so obviously that it seems it has materialized itself and is standing between me and them like an amorphous grey statue. All those whispered conversations concerning my legs; all the disdain I've always felt for my mates; all the failures in

153

my love life and those ominous predictions that I was never going to have one anyway; all those days when I was forbidden to bathe because of my monthly; all the hunger that can never be forgotten, all the brief mourning for my father, all the contempt I feel toward my mother – all of the above are less horrid than my brittle sterility. It has become a part of the grey shapeless statue that keeps growing and growing and hovering in front of me ... I know that I am gradually losing my mind.

I spend the days in front of my canvases filing my nails.

My nails are elegant. I like my nails. By nature they are almond-shaped, transparent and firm. Now I have let them grow very long and I spend hours working on them with a diamond file that sparks as it cuts thru twilight (I need no light to see what I'm doing). I want them to be pointed and sharp as a knife. I coated them with three layers of a transparent nail polish and they shine like ice. It seems to me that they have not sprouted from my flesh and blood (since I've stopped climbing roofs, my flesh and blood no longer give me pleasure) but were made by master jewelers – armourers, perhaps - for me to put on my fingers' ends like precious jewels not so much as an adornment but rather for me to enjoy looking at them and take pleasure from admiring them. I like the pain I feel each time I bury them into the hot flesh of my palm and clench my fist around them hard. I do like my finger-nails. They cut like razors. So efficient, they are.

I am surrounded by paintings. They are black, white and blue, and that is so beautiful. Still, something is missing. I am barren. The hatred I feel toward my own futility is barren. My barren hatred is growing into a rage. I would kill but the birds have flown south.

Then one gloomy evening I jump off my bed, stretch out my claws and leap on the closest canvas. It yields under my breasts (it is well stretched – I am a lousy painter but a good artisan) but doesn't tear. It is not, however, a match for my fingernails.

154

I raise my right arm high above my head and swing it toward my hip. The fingers of my left hand I simply plant into the fabric, suspend my whole body weight on them and wait for gravity to do the rest. The canvas is ripped in ten places but still adheres to the frame. The edges of the wounds are not tattered or serrated but smooth and clean as if disinfected. I destroy ten more paintings during the night.

And success is finally mine. When I read the critiques of my latest work it becomes clear to me that someone must be nuts here. Canvases ripped by fingernails are called by critics "an artistic paradigm in search of authentic, individualistic impression within a supertemporal transcendence, the ingenious expression of the subtle experience of the extrapolated." (Or the intrapolated, as you please.) "An ironic declaration of authentic femaleness and tenderness." (Huh!) "A socially engaged art. A call to a feminist intellectual revolution. A rejection of cliches on the basis of the classicist predetermination." And those least inventive satisfy themselves with a self-confident statement that here we are dealing with something completely new.

I paint and tear apart three or four canvases daily. I buy a fur coat for my mother. I try to convince Donovan to help me. He could layer paint – which is, at any rate, just the "embodied object of the painter's rebellion" – with his bushy tail. But he's far above getting himself dirty.

Donovan sits in front of the door, waiting patiently for someone to open it wide enough for his meter long white silky whiskers to pass through unimpeded. He's been waiting for four hours. When I push the door open he springs up and steps through as if in a hurry. But it's me who is in a hurry. In silk and pearls I am leaving for my first retrospective. I've succeeded. I've finally made it. Donovan and I wait together to cross the street in front of our house. He rubs himself against my ankle and steps onto the asphalt.

The cat is blind in one eye and does not see the oncoming truck. I scream and make a giant leap to pull him back. Too late. Just before the truck's front throws me into the air, just before I land with Donovan in my lap on its windshield, shattering it under my body, I realize that I have not really made it, and never will.

When I come to I am wrapped in something soft and warm, something that is alive, while something smelling of milk tickles my nose, making me sneeze funnily, several times. What I lie on trembles like a cello string, heaving like a friendly earthquake. I cannot open my eyes but I feel comforted and relaxed in the darkness that envelops me. I'm unable to decide whether to drink the milk in front of my nose or doze off again but I am certain that no matter what I decide it will turn out all right. I am safe. For the first time in my life I feel safe as sleep descends on me like a caressing hand.

Gently, someone lifts me up by the nape of my neck, turns me on my back and places me into something with softly rounded edges; perhaps it is a cradle, perhaps large cupped hands.

"It's a boy," a child's voice says.

As a matter of fact I am not, I want to say; but it really does not matter as long as I am allowed to sleep. Somehow I just know that here in this house I will be able to sleep to my heart's content.

"I'll call him Donovan," decides the child.

Translated by the author and Sonja Kravanja

Andrej E. Skubic

Andrej E. Skubic, born in 1967 in Ljubljana, has been publishing short stories in Slovenian literary magazines since 1990. His first novel, Grenki med (Bitter Honey), was published in 1999 and won the Kresnik award for best novel of the year in 2000, as well as the Slovenian Publishers and Booksellers prize for best first book. His second novel, Fužinski bluz (Fužine Blues), appeared in 2001 and was nominated for the Kresnik award the following year. It has been translated into Czech and Serbian and dramatised by the Slovenian National Theatre in 2005. In 2004, his first collection of short stories Norišnica (The Madhouse) was published to critical acclaim. His short stories have appeared in various literary magazines in English, Czech, Croatian, German, Hungarian, Polish and Russian. Skubic has translated a number of Irish and Scottish novels and anthologies. He is a freelance writer and lives in Ljubljana.

IT'S GOING TO BE ALRIGHT

Andrej E. Skubic

"And what did grandpa do then?" I ask. With one eye, I am trying to watch the television but it's a futile attempt. In her hands, Lana holds a picture book about a mouse and a hen who go swimming together. Her blue eyes are curious. They bore deep into my left ear. They are so very blue and so very serious. Jokes and evasion are crimes. "What does grandpa do?" I ask again, though a bit absentmindedly. Enthusiasm is not necessary; participation is. Anyhow the main news stories are already over. Grandpa is also not exactly enthusiastic about Lana's interpretation of this story, though it does indicate a certain progress in her imagination. According to her explanation of the picture book, I am the mouse who inflates the little pool and Lana is the hen who fills the pool with water. The fact that the mouse in the picture book possesses – in addition to an enormous nose and a moustache and a purple shirt – a tail, none of which I have, puzzles her a little. Though not too much. Indeed she persists that I, her da-da, also have a tail *in reality*; she just doesn't know how to find it yet. But that's only a minor problem. I sometimes wonder how other people find their place in the universe. I'm not sure at all. I think that

159

probably in her eyes I am some sort of pathetic copy of the real thing, of the perfect da-da who has the essential and true nature of da-da-ism, who is the way a da-da should be with all the necessary accessories including an impressive tail that can be waved magnificently in the air, a tail like our ancestors once had, a great species that has degenerated over time. When I ride Lana on my bicycle, she likes to lift my tee shirt and run her finger along my tailbone in hopes of discovering the long concealed organ. "Gegi boom boom!" Lana shouts triumphantly. When the pool is filled, an elephant named Gaspar wearing enormous swimming trunks enters the scene and throws himself into the water so that there is no room for either the mouse or the hen. That is the dramatic climax of the story. It seems to me that it is Lana's interpretation of this part of the story that gets on grandpa's nerves. Why does grandpa have to be the *elephant*? There are much more interesting animals in the story. He wouldn't have to be a lion or anything – he wouldn't exaggerate – but there are ostriches and badgers ...

"Boom boom!"

Lana throws herself butt-first into the pool making the water splash on all sides. Fuck this kind of swimming. This health spa swimming. I don't understand the benefits of it, even for pensioners. What do they see in spas? In wintertime, let alone summer?

There are hordes of people here. Everybody lolling around in a murky puddle that is nearly ninety degrees. They look totally relaxed, giving the impression that that's the whole point, that it's normal to get a little *wet* when it's hot outside. That you can take the heat easier. As much as I understand it, when it's hot, getting *wet* means getting *refreshed*, or something like that.

A tepid liquid from the bosom of mother earth squirted on to hundreds of sweaty homo sapiens who have achieved a level of intelligence that dictates that they soak in hot water in the middle of summer. I mean – what is the point of it? And yet here I am with the rest of them, lying on my stomach in the kiddy pool. I prop myself up on my elbows and my wet ponytail coils damply around my neck. What luxury.

Well, Lana gets it. For Lana, warm water in the hottest season of the year doesn't pose any problem – hey, it's water. Her bluish water wings glitter. Grinning broadly, she thrusts her chin up and forward. Klara is lying on her stomach on the other side of the pool, smiling at Lana. Who wouldn't? I don't know why I feel such pressure in my stomach.

"Look," I whisper to Lana. "Mommy's a fish. She looks toward her mother with amazement. "Mommy not," she says. And then: "Not f-f-f."

Outside, behind the thick glass that separates the indoor pool from the outdoor one, the sky is dark gray. We will soon see the first flash of lighting. Two tall cranes stand outside the pool. If one of them were struck by lightning it would be a real spectacle, maybe even dangerous. Has anyone ever been electrocuted in a swimming pool at a health spa? Or what about all of the thousands of sweaty occupants at once? That would be something.

Outside there is a soft stifled rumble. Lana winces and looks over her shoulder, across the back of the armchair, and then at me. The booming in the sky above us drags on: it is far away enough that the echoes fan outward, far outward, hundreds of meters. Lana has an expectant look on her face. Da-da?

"Is that thunder?" I say. I turn my head slightly – I don't feel like turning my whole body. Yeah, a storm's coming. Night is slowly falling, but it's darker than it would be if everything were normal. On our side of the house, you can't see that many clouds. Probably they are directly above us, above the roof of the building, already pretty black. The darkening air in front of the window doesn't look sinister, just a bit sorrowful.

161

"Yeah," says Lana.

The leaves outside flutter, moved by a light wind. Lana looks at me and sort of smiles.

With an awkward hand, Lana tears the dandelion stem and gives me a sassy look. We are standing in tall grass, right beside the edge of a hay field. Klara stands on slightly higher ground, about thirty meters away, beside the bench where we have our bag, camera and snack. It's a pretty afternoon. The view is magnificent even though we're not that high up. On one side, we can see all the way to Nazarje, Bona ob Dreti, Nova Štifta, and on the other side, the mountain massif of Robanov kot. A little lower, about three hundred meters away, a house can be seen, a big farmhouse, some kind of agricultural tourism. It's in a nice setting, though it looks like it might need more infrastructure. There's no children's playground, for example. There was a time when I didn't think about that sort of thing. The forest behind us. It's a bit hazy, the sky a gray veil. It's also a bit cooler now, which is actually fine. We've had enough heat. This is ideal for Lana.

"Aaaaayyyy!" She tickles my bare leg with the dandelion stem. I feel a little stupid but I start hopping around: that's my role, the convention of such things. I respect that. Lana tickles me. Lana tickles da-da. Lana smiles broadly. Lana is in a brilliant mood. It's strange but when I look at her it seems to me that, despite her happiness, her regard is unusually dull. Suspiciously dull.

*

"Is it funny?" I ask her, and turn my head a little more. Yeah, the wind has started to blow: a storm is definitely on the way.

"Yeah," says Lana and puts down the picture book. She pulls herself up slowly and grabs the back of the couch and looks outside. A sudden blast of wind and the leaves on the tree

162

shudder; the window is closed but you can almost feel the rustling of the maples. Though I bet that's only a poetic illusion because the windows are new, plastic and sealed five times so those kind of wild natural sounds haven't got a chance of getting in. Lana watches the leaves enthusiastically.

"Da-da!" she cries, pointing at the silverish bottom side of the leaves that are alternately revealed in the oscillating branches.

"What is it, Lana?" I say, and look up to see if the blackness has actually covered the sky right above us, or if there's still some chance that the clouds will roll on.

"Aa," says Lana indecisively.

"Do you want to tell me something?" As usual, a short instance of silence follows this question. Lana hugs the back of the couch and stares outside.

"Yeah," she says after a while.

I watch her from the side. Her profile has a meditative outline that is still quite easy to make out in the strange half dusk.

"Daddy also wants you to tell him something," I say. She turns toward me, smiles, and then leans in. Her warm little fingertips hold my face. She presses my face to her cheeks, almost to her mouth. Soft tiny lips. The softest lips on earth.

"Would you like me to pick a leaf for you?" I ask.

Lana wades with powerful steps through the water. Or rather, her steps give the impression of power because they swagger here and there though, in truth, she is on the verge of falling down the whole time. She smiles with her whole face. Her light blue bathing gown flaps loosely around her. And then her smile stiffens for an instant, her eyes go astray, and her steps become uncertain. Only for a second, but enough to make my stomach tighten. But then she is smiling again, standing at the edge of the deep end, and she moves on. Klara and I look at each other. We are both thinking exactly the same thing. There is no doubt. Our experiences are so common and so exhausting.

163

It isn't possible that one of us would be thinking anything else. But everything's all right. It only lasted a second and we are used to such seconds. It's no problem to live with them. Warm water splashes everywhere. Maybe it's too warm; that could be a problem. She can't get too warm. It's a disaster, a fucking disaster, if she gets too warm.

"Yaaa," she sings. I have to laugh. The leaves under the window tremble in the stronger gusts. In the street below, little eddies of dust hurry here and there across the asphalt. Maybe there'll be a hailstorm; the conditions are just right for one. Klara's in the city. God knows where she parked the car. It could get all dented up again. We've been through that before.

"Lana," I say, "Daddy can't pick a leaf for you. It's too far away."

Lana stands up and looks a little confused. It seems that her blue eyes are asking why I offered in the first place. Da-da, we agreed that that you wouldn't lead me on like that.

"Daddy would fall down to the street if he reached for a leaf," I say, trying to get myself off the hook.

Again the questioning look.

"Boom-boom," I try to explain with more understandable words. Lana smiles, resting one arm on the back of the couch. The smile becomes rigid and the hand on the back of the couch tightens, the elbow shudders. Her gaze suddenly shifts to the right, then the whole face. I know in that instant.

Lana's face is utterly inscrutable as she tickles my bare legs with the dandelion stem. She smiles and watches me but it is as if she doesn't see me. Her eyes seem to be fixed a millimeter to the left of where I actually am. They are focused maybe ten centimeters farther away from where I am actually standing. But she just keeps smiling and throwing the shredded dandelion flower toward me. I don't know what to think. She's so happy. It was never like this before. I squat down. She is

164

actually looking past me. And her smile is fading. Her eyes are serious, pensive.

"Lana," I say to her, "can you look at daddy?"

"No," she says thoughtfully. She's still talking. It's unbelievable.

"Lana," I ask, "do you feel bad?" Lana's gaze shifts even more to the right, but she's still standing, still answering.

"Yes," she says.

She topples in the water like a fallen tree. It's completely unambiguous, but because I'm lying on my stomach in the warm water, I can't get up immediately to help. It is like those dreams when you try to run but you can't. Flailing my arms, I try to stand up, to splash forward, toward her. Her little head with the flowered swimming cap sways under the tiny waves of the spa pool like a duck. Thank god her head is twisted back. Before she fell, her arms had been stretched forward and upward, in a gesture of prayer, and now that she is horizontal, they have hardened in that position and lifted her chin out of the water. From behind her, you can hardly see that she is moving slightly: up and down, up and down.

I plunge forward suddenly on the couch and grab her. I have her in my arms but I can't stop it: she cries softly, already retreating, far away. Each second there is less of her. There is no force on earth that can stop her. Her lips curl, one more small moan, and then she is zipped up. Gone.

*

I throw myself toward her as quickly as the slippery floor allows. It's as if I'm in slow motion. Time – and it is probably only a question of seconds – seems to disperse into countless fragments that scatter around the entire pool: to the farthest bathers sprawling happily in the water, to the ones in the café sipping coca-cola or licking an ice cream cone, to the ones lying around on lounges, on towels, comfortable and warm. Great. Good for them. I already have her in my arms. I hold her under her armpits. She's stiff, her hands awkward. She thrusts slowly upward like an overturned toy in which some part of the mechanism is stuck and the wheel just keeps mercilessly turning, trying to move her forward. But she's not going anywhere. I don't even need to see her to know. I know she's looking straight up with white porcelain eyes. I know because both of the armpits I support with my palms are shaking in exactly the same way which means that both hemispheres of her brain are convulsing. I know that both of her little legs are turned slightly inward, that they are taut but powerless. I know all of this just as I know that Klara is rushing toward our bag next to the chaise lounge, that her eyes are wide open but concentrated, concentrated by the adrenaline.

When I lay her on the couch, she looks like a corpse. Her eyes are turned to the right, unmoving, like those of a dead animal. They are very dark, fixed on some other place. God knows what she sees. I've often wracked my brain with that. It's no wonder that it was once called the divine malady. When it begins, the body stiffens as if in ecstasy, as if the divine in all its magnificence is slowly being revealed. The face grows gradually bluish, the lower lip clamps convulsively and slowly, slowly, almost imperceptibly, comes the rhythmical movement – up, down, up, down. Maybe she is seeing da-da with his powerful tail. I don't know. I hold her by her shoulders and look at her.

"Lana?" I say. "Lana?"

I want to tell her something else, though I don't know what, something that would help, something she could hear. And though I kiss her softly, her warm shuddering shoulder, prick it with my stubble, it doesn't matter: she's gone. Her eyes are the worst – I don't know where they're looking. When I hold her, my fingers go right through her.

Klara and I lay her on the bench by the meadow. Lana is utterly away and when we stand in front of her, we don't know if she sees us or not. She's alone, confused, unhappy. Her breathing is shallow, her face faintly blue, but not very, not very. What does that mean? Is it a full-fledged attack or not? Would a small squirt of midazalom under her cheek help? She wouldn't like it. She's still partially conscious and she might swallow it and that's not good. It has to be absorbed slowly through the mucous membrane, through the capillaries and into the blood, and then to her brain where her neurons are sending 3 Hz jolts to another part of the brain tissue. It could wipe out someone much larger, let alone a tiny little two-year old who just sits there and looks more and more to the left. But that's what's happening. She is looking away from the magnificent view of Nazarje, beyond Bona ob Dreti and Nova Štifta, toward Robanov Kot to the north. The sky is hazy and heavy. She is starting to breath more evenly. Veliki Rogatec is a ragged cliff tearing at the belly of the air. Lana's eyebrows faintly, almost imperceptibly, begin to twitch, up down, up down.

There's no time left: she's too blue. Soon two minutes will have passed and she can't take more than that. But I must be calm. I take a tiny plastic bottle from the box. On the bottom there's a tube and on the top a long conical neck with a round cap at the tip. Stesolid, ten milligrams of diazepam. Street kids wash the same stuff down with a gulp of wine. It makes them feel good. It'll make this little creature feel good too. In the box, there is also a small tube of lubricating gel. I open it and squeeze a little bit on the end of my forefinger. Then I toss it back on the table with the box. I have only the plastic bottle in my hand. I quickly lubricate the conical neck of the bottle. Then I grab the little cap and twist it, breaking it off. We're ready.

I pull down Lana's pants and diaper. Her bottom looks so tiny next to the big diaper. When I grab her and somehow adjust her bottom, Lana shudders. It's strange. I could swear she is completely unconscious, but it's as if a little piece of her is still here. She's here and listening when I call out her name.

"Lana," I say, "Lana." When I push the tip of the tube into her tiny anus, she begins to shudder again as is she wants to get away from it. But she can't because she is zipped up and somewhere else, not here where her body is, the body that I am about to penetrate with this tiny plastic tube. "Lana," I say, "Daddy's going to give you medicine now, so you'll feel better." I know that the words don't help. I know that explanations mean nothing. But she is no longer resisting, probably because she isn't here anymore though she almost seemed to be before. But now it is certain. Now all that it is left are the trembling muscles of the person I love most in the world.

I push the tube halfway in and press.

There are three older men in the jacuzzi next to us. The one who is facing us has his eyes closed. How long will it last? If it lasts too long, she's in trouble. Klara is leaning over her, holding her head and whispering in her ear. Lana is shaking as if she were hooked up to an electric circuit. She already got a milliliter of midazalom. It should kick in soon. If it doesn't in five minutes, we'll give her another half, and if that doesn't work there's nothing left we can do to help her. The ampoule I'm holding in my hand feels as hard as a piece of wire. There's too much water in this place, too much warm water. If a thing like this lasts too long, calcium and water enter the brain in quantities that are dangerous to the neurons and begin to break into our memories and all that we are. There's too much water. It releases glutamate and that opens the doors to even more calcium. The neurons become more and more agitated and begin to throb, they pulse to the rhythm of all those ions and electrons and quarks and shake her entire body that rotates along with the planet Earth. All the calcium releases even more glutamate and the doors open wider and wider and the water washes away everything: the apartment, the furniture, the playground, the photos in the album, da-da's computer, the toys. If it last much longer, it will wash away the name da-da. And last of all, I figure it will also wash away the name mama. It will wash away everything. Frog will run to Duck but Duck's house will already be underwater. Together they will run to Pig but Pig will already be looking out the attic window of his flooded house. Then they will all run in front of the flood until they come to Hare whose house is on a hill, safe from the raging waters. There they will eat together. Hare has spinach and carrots and apples and bread, but one day he sees that he only has one more loaf of bread and that will soon be gone too.

The couch bites into my knee. Her terrible black look, the wide-open lids, the gaze directed all the way to the right so that most of the eyes appears completely white like a hot milky sky and above it darkness and airlessness. The universe rotates like her eyes: Venus, Jupiter, asteroids, quasars, and black holes. All of it slides over to one side and then departs. I watch her: Lana's hands slowly begin to shake, then stronger jerks. That could be a good sign, or it could not. The clonic phase usually doesn't last long. I just hope she doesn't stay in a state of absence. Her seizures are incredibly complex, more complex than any handbook indicates. Lana beats all the handbooks. The soft skin on her legs rubs against my cheeks. All of her is shaking.

"Lana," I say. "Lana."

Then suddenly: a momentary stiffening. I lift my head sharply. She stiffens, moans loudly, and lets out a breath. I think I also let out a breath. As if a massive avalanche has been displaced. She exhales again. Oh god.

Lana closes her eyes. Oh god. She closes her eyes and breathes. Inhales, exhales. The exhalation is strained, moaning, but it's going to be alright. It's going to be alright. In fact,

169

it's going to be wonderful. Her eyes are closed, her face re-laxed. There's saliva around her lips, but it's going to be alright. Yes, it's going to be alright.

I lie on the couch.

Outside the wind still howls and drops of rain lash the glass, but that's alright too. The discarded little box, the emptied rectal tube, the broken cap on the table next to the remote control, the wrinkled magazine, the yellow plastic bowl with the little red ladle. The anchorman on the television news is still talking about the defeat of the women's handball team. The book about the mouse and the hen is on the floor, and the little elephant that reminds her of grandpa. It's alright, Lana. Even if a storm rages outside and the hail falls down on everything. It's going to be alright.

I just lie there and close my eyes. My thoughts slowly spool away from me. It was the same the other time as well, on the plastic lounge chair beside the pool. She rasped and exhaled, moaned and cried. She usually doesn't cry, but it was alright, and then for a couple of minutes she couldn't fall asleep though she was completely wiped out from the shaking – there was too much noise around her. She asked for her pacifier but we didn't have it with us. Finally she fell asleep without it. Even above that spectacular view of Nazarje, toward Robanov Kot, she eventually closed her eyes and sighed. Her body relaxed and she breathed to the time of dreams, nothing both-ered her, not the clouds or anything else. It had lasted twenty minutes, but it had ended. I dream the ending, I only dream the endings, I dream that she exhales, I dream the air in her lungs and the song about the sun and the moon and the twinkling stars: peace.

I am probably half dreaming when I feel as if I am reaching my hand outside the window, out into the darkness and the cold and the rain, reaching out to pluck a glittering wet leave that is

170

desperately dancing in the blows of the wind and the rain. My hand stiffens and I can only feel the hateful sky, the damned hateful sky that lashes my skin, and then I feel it less and my palm is almost like wood, and then I don't feel much at all anymore. The glittering leave evades me in the pale light, I'll never get it, it comes close and then retreats in icy disdain, it's playing with me, and my face sinks into the spray of raindrops, my eyes almost completely closed from the whipping they're taking, and then completely closed. How can the clouds do such a thing to me, I wonder, when at the very edge of my rigid hand that has gone almost completely numb I suddenly feel the kind softness of her small warm searching fingers holding my wrist, and I clasp them and I pull her inside.

Translated by Erica Johnson Debeljak

Jani Virk

Jani Virk, *born in 1962 in Ljubljana, studied German and contemporary literature. He writes novels and short stories, and also translates from German. He has worked as editor of a number of magazines and newspapers; currently he works for the Slovene National Television as Head of Cultural Programmes. He was awarded the Prešeren Fund prize for literature. His best known books are Rahela (novel), Sergij's Last Temptation (novel), Arythmia (novel), The Door and Other Stories (collection of short stories), Looking at Tycho Brahe (collection of short stories) and Laughter Behind a Wooden Fence (novel). His work has been translated into a number of languages.*

ON THE BORDER

Jani Virk

He knew it would happen once. He knew very well. But he was sorry he hadn't brought a knife or a gun. When he went into the village in the evening, he almost always carried a weapon in the jacket pocket, although he sometimes had trouble with the police. Across the narrow macadam road leading to his estate there stood a cart loaded with lumber; a van drove onto the road behind him and put the long lights on. He stopped; he couldn't go on, he couldn't turn back. He knew it was them, his neighbours, the five brothers. He opened the door, jumped out of the jeep and ran towards the forest; among the dark silhouettes of the trees he saw a way out, but there was no way out. He heard a dog barking before him, and a moment later the dog rushed onto him; with his elbow he tried to hit its jaws and managed to duck the bite, but lost his balance. As he was falling over he heard nervous steps and an instant later felt a hollow pain in his neck. "Not on the head, not on the head," a voice came from the dark, he knew the voice, rolled into the foetal position and manoeuvered among the kicks and blows with a stick, somebody hit him on the face with a shoe, warm blood ran over his lips; suddenly he didn't feel the pain any more; as he rolled over the ground he managed to grab a stone, picked it up and threw it at the closest of the brothers. There was a numb heavy sound of a blow and a painful cry; he thumped around him until he collapsed under the blows and lost consciousness.

Although he was lying motionless on the ground, they kept kicking and hitting him with sticks, until one of them said: "We must've killed him, let's stop." In the warm spring night one could hear their gurgling breath, the moon was shining onto the motionless man on the ground, his face stuck in the sparse grass beside the road. "We killed him," the male voice repeated and broke into nervous, convulsive laughter, "we killed him, he got what he deserved."

They took hold of his body and dragged him towards the car, placed him by the wheel, his head hit the windscreen, they closed the door, he fell over the seats, somewhere far behind he perceived a tiny spot of consciousness, which was his consciousness, he saw himself lying covered in blood over the seats, blood oozing out of his mouth; he inhaled, through the thick sticky liquid a slender waft of fresh air entered his lungs, he heard somebody open the trunk of his jeep, he smelt petrol and then burning plastic, from the back seats burst the crackling tongues of flame, pink light penetrated through his lids to the eyes, through his memory flashed the image of his dying father lying trapped under the tractor, vomiting blood during his final breaths. "The fight is over now," he whispered to himself through his swollen lips, "I'm crossing over, I'll run down the riverbed of life and sink into the soil." He heard the metallic murmur of the engine, the brothers were driving back along the road, "bastards, they've beaten me," he thought and breathed in the thick, lumpy, suffocating smoke, "soon I'll be the light of the flame, the fiery grain in the embrace of darkness, I'll dissolve into the air, rub myself into the smell of pine

176

needles and the feathers of jackdaws." Before his eyes flashed the vision of his estate, the herd of livestock, the pack of mad dogs, the graves of his parents at the edge of the forest, "everything will fall apart," he thought, "everything will be overgrown by woods." He stretched his hand towards the door and hit the glass with the knuckles of his fingers, lowered the fingers to the handle, hooked his middle and ring fingers into it, but didn't have enough strength to open the door; he gasped for breath in the gooey mixture of blood and thick smoke, he put his free hand on his belly and tried to raise himself onto his knees, he was choking, and in the desperate gasping for life he managed to gather enough strength to push himself with his knees towards the door and shift the handle; he thrust his head against the door and swayed his body out into the fresh spring night. With the remnants of his strength he rolled out of the vehicle, fell onto the sharp gravel and, sinking back into unconsciousness, instinctively rolled into the ditch.

An explosion resounded into the night, and echoed from the membranes of the hills; parts of the vehicle flew into the air and were falling onto the road and the trees in the light of the moon. His body jerked at the blow, but he didn't reawaken; he lay in the ditch on his hip, the blood, which had oozed from his mouth, was coagulating on his cheeks, from his forehead the warm blood was still slowly dripping across his closed eyelids. He didn't know where he was, he wasn't thinking about who he was, he levitated in the matter lighter than water and heavier than air, fibre-like layers peeled off huge white pillars, splashed around and reassembled themselves into new pillars, everything was in the state of disintegrating and re-emerging, no living being anywhere, only the murmuring whirlpools of formless life, flakes of flowing energy, the pure light of the kind of being he didn't know. He heard the voice of his mother, a silent, gentle soothing which he didn't understand, her caressing voice, soft touches of her formless lips, the sprinkle of her warm breath without any smell. He hovered light and translucent, flaky white tissue among the changing forms, he was dissolving and rejoining, and yet he remained always the same, always different and always himself in the extendible and indestructible spot of consciousness.

The van drove down the dusty macadam road, jumping. Two of the brothers had smashed faces; the stone had crushed the lip of the youngest and knocked out some teeth. Leaning onto the window he whimpered and hissed through his swollen mouth.

"We should've tortured him slowly," he said.

"No," somebody else said. "It's enough we killed him."

"No," somebody else said. "We should've knocked all his teeth out with stones and then done him in slowly."

"No," somebody else said, "We did the right thing. He's dead, and this is all that matters."

"No," somebody else said, "we should've killed him gradually, piece by piece, we should be torturing him now. We did away with him too quickly. Now he's dead and he doesn't suffer any more, but the little one will have to put up with the empty spaces between his teeth for life."

"And he'll be dead for life, which is worse," somebody else said and laughed with a coarse cough.

"What are we going to say at home?" somebody else asked.

"We'll say that he hit our lumber cart and that his jeep caught fire," somebody else said.

"Yes," somebody else said and laughed heavily, distortedly, "it's not our fault that it happened."

"Yes," somebody else said, "it's not our fault. He was asking for it. He'd pestered us for too long."

When the van stopped before the homestead, the light was still on in the kitchen although it was well after midnight. Two of the brothers grabbed the youngest by the armpits and they entered the

178

house. In the kitchen the father was sleeping in his wheelchair, and the mother and sister were putting plates on the table. When she saw them, the mother stopped; she noticed two bloody faces.

"What happened?" she asked.

"A tree fell and got them," said the eldest.

"Why didn't you bring them home earlier?" she asked.

"It happened when we were almost done," he replied, "it was pitch dark; we didn't know it was that bad. They wanted us to finish. They were still able to help."

"And then we wanted to put out the cart," somebody else said. "The neighbour came by and crashed into it."

The father, an old man of eighty, with red eyes, confused from age and the sleep he'd just woken up from, looked vacantly around. He raised himself in the wheelchair, the metal screeched, everybody looked towards him.

"What happened to him?" he snarled with a hoarse, rude voice at his sons.

"He was burnt," said one of the brothers.

"You didn't help?" asked the old man.

"No," said the eldest.

"You did right," said the old man, "this is what happens to those who stand in our way. It took too long. It's too late for me. You rejoice."

With eyes red from the thick web of capillaries he scanned the room, nobody dared interrupt his look with words. He smiled contemptuously, and then his head drooped on his shoulder and he went back to sleep.

"You killed him," said the mother. "Why don't you tell him that you killed him, it would make him happy."

"We didn't kill him, mama," said the eldest, "they could lock us up if we killed him, you know. He killed himself, he was burnt and we didn't help him, that's all. I told you, he crashed into our cart, into our lumber. It's all his fault."

"Yes, it's his fault" somebody else said.

She didn't believe them, but it didn't matter. All that mattered was that the young neighbour was dead and there would be peace for a while.

"Klara, take father to bed," she said to the daughter, "I'll serve them."

The daughter loosened the safety brake on the wheelchair and pushed the father out of the kitchen. He was snoring; it sounded as if rusty saw-teeth were sliding loosely and screechily along wet wood. Klara hated her father, was afraid of him yet admired him. Although he'd been confined to the wheelchair for five years, nothing on the farm or in the forest happened without him. He knew every tree, every span of the land, every animal on his property. He knew people, he knew his sons, he knew that – him being an invalid – they'd rush at him and do away with him if he didn't intimidate and keep them at bay with the story about pounds of gold. Twenty years he'd spent in Australia, he returned at forty, bought a young girl through an advert and fathered six children. From abroad he brought back quite a lot of money he'd saved and invested it into his estate and purchase of the neighbouring land. Everybody gave in; if necessary, he paid three times more than the land was worth. Only with the old neighbour was there trouble; no wonder he was killed by a tractor, his sons saw how the tractor tripped over and buried him underneath, and then there was trouble only with the young neighbour; no wonder he crashed into a pile of timber, his sons had seen how he crashed into a pile of timber.

"They think I'm asleep," he mumbled half-napping, when his daughter was wheeling him out of the kitchen. Thick brown nicotine saliva dribbled from his mouth as from a dog's jaws. "They're trembling with fear that I might die without telling them where the chunks of gold are buried, hyenas! They'll rip

180

my tongue out of my mouth when I die and don't tell them anything," he mumbled through his clenched teeth. He smiled to himself, there were no chunks of gold anywhere, although he kept saying he'd brought them decades ago from Australia and hidden them somewhere on the estate. All he had brought was a lump of ore with some glittering traces of gold, and the lump now stood motionless on the mantelpiece like a promise of wealth and power; the sons were humbly passing by it bowing to their father, to the one who knew, to the one who'd bequeath a fortune to them and make them happy.

"Now the road's open," said the eldest son in the kitchen. "We won't have to drive around any more."

"Yes," somebody else said, "we'll cut the wires and pull down the gate."

"We'll shoot his dogs," somebody else said.

"No, we'll poison them," somebody else said.

"We'll slaughter his livestock and sell it," somebody else said.

"We'll level the graves of his parents," somebody else said, "we'll suffer none of them by our side, living or dead."

The mother watched them proudly, her sons. "They've grown into real men," she was thinking, "they're so hard and brave, and yet so soft towards me and father. God knows they aren't bad, only life up here is hard. God knows they're actually good and humble, but they have some of their father's hot blood in them."

"What do you think, they killed him, right?" he asked Klara, when she wheeled him to the bed. His head rested on his shoulder as if his neck were broken; it gave her the shudders. "He's sleeping and talking," she thought, "he's dead and talking."

"I don't know," she said quietly and thought of the neighbour. She hated him, as her entire family hated him, but she hated him differently. After she'd finished primary school down in the valley four years ago, she was never alone among unknown people. She worked on the farm and only every now and then

181

went shopping with her brothers. She was seeing new faces mostly on TV, they had a satellite dish up on the roof, a huge white plate, and on Saturdays she usually watched programmes late into the night, in English, which she hardly understood. The fresh corpse her father was talking about was familiar; she often watched him, his estate was beneath theirs, and although there was a strip of forest along the stream, which separated the two farms, she could easily see his from their barn. She knew the neighbour's face well, although she never saw him quite up close. She remembered how she and her brothers used to watch him from the barn through the telescopic sight of the rifle, and sometimes aimed just above his head at the tin roof of his house or hit one of his animals. She, too, sometimes crept to the barn and watched him through binoculars; he had a better stature than her brothers, was almost always clean-shaven, and when he was wearing his denim overalls and a flannel shirt he reminded her, with his broad face and strong teeth, of the man from a TV commercial for blue jeans, and sometimes she felt a gentle shiver in her body and her hand slid down her body and stopped in the soft, warm shrub under her belly. She didn't know whether it was right, she often felt disgusted at herself afterwards, she hated the man across the border, she hated him because she had to hate him, everybody in her family hated him, and yet it sometimes seemed that when she looked at him the warm shrub under the belly was set on fire, and she couldn't, didn't want to resist the sensation. Sometimes she took her sewing and knitting up to the barn, and then she kept looking over towards him, watching him work in the field, feed his animals and throw his wild dogs chunks of bloody meat. She also saw that occasionally he spread a piece of canvas between wooden poles and painted for hours. It seemed ridiculous to her, nobody in her house ever did anything like it; through the binoculars she watched the colours on the canvas and felt good inside. "It's pretty," the thought rushed though her mind, "funny, what this man is doing," she whispered to herself. It sometimes happened that one of her brothers noticed that the neighbour had forgotten to hide the drying canvas behind the house, and he pierced the painting with lead bullets. She always laughed; she carried in her veins the hatred towards the handsome neighbour who was making their life bitter. She openly hated and covertly admired him for daring to resist them all by himself; sometimes, feeling enraged at him, when he perforated their milk canisters, when he beat up one of the brothers down in the valley or when his dogs slaughtered one of their animals, she was thinking how she would scratch the skin on his clean-shaven, pretty face with her nails, and shivered with the deep, sensuous desire to do it.

She put her father to bed, covered his fat, old body and crept out of the house.

He felt a wet prickle on his face; he opened his eyes and through the aching swellings saw his St. Bernard licking his face. The morning sun was shining, mist was rising from the ground in pale, milky waves. With difficulty he moved his head, looked around, he couldn't remember what had happened, then it dawned on him. "The neighbours," he sighed. His entire body ached, he moved his hand, it slid along the thick shaggy cloth; he looked down at his body. During the night somebody had covered him with a blanket, he didn't dwell on the thought who that might have been – he didn't know anybody who'd do that for him. He grabbed the dog round the neck and sat up, felt a piercing pain in his ribs, coughed and spat out some coagulated blood. On the road he saw a heap of metal and the remains of car tyres. "There would be nothing left of me," he mumbled, "perhaps a tooth on the macadam, a button among the shrubs along the road." His body was nothing but a mass of pain, yet he stood up, picked up a dry pole from the grass and staggered down the road. His legs were shaking; after a few steps he stopped before the logs lying across the road, leaned onto the pole and tried to raise his leg high, but couldn't, he felt a twist, fell over across the logs and hit the wood hard with his shoulder. He remained lying on his back and stared into the clear sky; he was familiar with the feeling of helplessness, once, when he was ski-touring in the mountains, he was swept away in an avalanche and buried underneath it, and although in his mind had given in he felt such a strong desire to live after a few minutes that he couldn't resist it and so to speak against his plans dug himself from under the snow and dragged himself down to the valley with a broken leg. The sun was hurting his eyes, after a while he propped his feet on the logs, rolled over onto his belly, shifted his body across the logs and stood up. "This is not the end yet," he mumbled, "not the end yet," he repeated and, hardly managing to stand up, stumbled towards his home only a couple of hundred metres away.

When he unlocked the chain and walked through the large screeching gate of his estate, the pack of his dogs came rushing towards him. He stood there, leaning against the fence; they jumped up to him, knocked him over, licked his coagulated blood and snarled. "They'll attack me," he thought, "they'll fight for their master, tear him apart in their blind bloody beastly love." He wasn't afraid; through the slit of his swollen lids he watched their blood-shot, hungry, devoted eyes, the drizzle of their saliva, the glittering of their fur in the morning sun. He was calling their names and touching their sharp teeth with his hand. "In this world the only loyal creatures are the animals," he thought in his aching and dizzy head, then he whistled sharply; the dogs rushed to the house and sat down on the steps. He pulled himself up and tripped into the house, took a couple of chunks of raw meat from the fridge and threw them out. He had no strength to go to the bathroom and look at his beaten face; he dragged himself to the bed, fell into it and immediately went to sleep.

In the afternoon he was awoken by fierce barking, he got up quickly and whimpered with pain, slithered to the window and heard the shooting. He knew where it was coming from; he took hold of his rifle and opened the window. The brothers were standing in the grove behind his fence and the electric wire, shooting at his dogs, he could see two of them lying motionless on the ground; he lifted his rifle and started shooting towards the neighbours. Never before had he aimed straight at them, but now he didn't care what would happen if he killed them. He heard them shouting, somebody was yelling and rolling on the ground. He knew he'd hit one, he was aiming at the man lying on the ground, he was a sitting duck; he pulled the trigger and paused for an instant. He felt hatred within, breathed in the air through the nostrils, the inflated ribs hurt, he felt like porcelain just before it breaks. He shot into the air, into the treetops, none of the brothers dared approach the wounded one, sobbing and holding his shoulder.

Silence filled with suspense hung above the landscape, he watched the young woman running from the neighbouring farm towards the border; he knew she was the sister, he'd met her down in the village a couple of times, when she came shopping with her brothers. She had a nice figure, large breasts, in the old days, when he was just over twenty, he used to like that kind of women. It was all in the past; he hadn't had a woman for years, and didn't miss one. "That would be a nice revenge," he thought and watched the woman aiming at her with the gun. He heard the brothers screaming, they wanted to stop her getting to the wounded one, but she ran there nevertheless and leaned over him; his hands were shaking, he closed his eyes and imagined how he'd pulled the trigger, he pictured the flight of the bullet through the warm spring air and a tiny dribble of blood on the young woman's forehead. No; he couldn't shoot her, he opened his eyes and saw the girl dragging her brother towards the forest, he became aware of his two shot dogs in the field, sent another bullet into the air and went back to bed.

The wounded brother was dragged to the house; he was moaning and breathing deeply.

"Somebody hit him in the shoulder," the eldest brother said to the father sitting in the wheelchair before the entrance.

"And what did you do to him?" asked the old man.

"Nothing," the eldest replied, "we were out in the open, and he was hiding in the house."

The old man swung the stick, but didn't reach him.

"Idiots! Who do you think it was, eh?" he hissed towards his sons with a voice, which broke into a rattling whisper.

"It wasn't him," somebody said, "yesterday he was burnt in the car."

"We soaked him in petrol and set him alight," somebody said.

"I went to check today," somebody said, "there was nothing left of him, just a heap of metal."

"We beat him to death and burnt him," somebody said, "we all saw he was dead."

"Yesterday you said you didn't kill him," the old man groaned.

"We killed him, father," said the eldest.

"We killed him," somebody else repeated.

"You didn't kill him," the old man said silently, ominously. "Now it'll start all over again." From under the blanket covering his legs he pulled out a gun, raised the shaking hand and shot towards the neighbour's estate until he ran out of bullets.

The wounded brother was carried into the house, Klara watched the brothers trying to take the bullet out of his shoulder. She thought of the neighbour, she was sorry she'd covered him with a blanket during the night, "I should've told them I

186

found him alive in the ditch," she thought, but didn't dare speak up.

"We'll have to take him down to the valley," the eldest said.

"What will we say?" somebody asked.

"Nothing," said the eldest, "a hunting accident."

"We'll strike back," somebody said.

"Yes, we'll strike back," somebody said.

"This time we'll kill him," somebody said.

"We've killed him already," somebody said.

"No, we didn't kill him," somebody said. "It was him in the house, the old man's right. Who else could it be?"

"We'll wait a few days, then we'll burn the house," somebody said.

"Yes," the eldest said, "it's too much. We'll do it."

They put the brother into the van and took him to the village. The father gazed sharply after them, he was holding a cigarette between his lips, his face was all yellow from nicotine, it had been long since he stopped holding the cigarette with his hands, he'd light one and hold it between the lips, the ashes dropping onto the cardigan and blanket, nicotine saliva dribbling from the corners of his mouth. He didn't feel sorry for his wounded son; for him, the children were like his livestock – part of the estate, part of his property. "I did everything," he gurgled to himself, "I bought everything myself, they're only waiting for me to croak. But I won't; I'll survive them," he said stubbornly, "I'll survive them all." His head dropped onto his chest, the daughter watched him with a mixture of fear and pity, she stepped closer and took the smouldering butt from his mouth. He wasn't asleep, he knew it was her, "Klara is all I've got," he thought to himself, tears gathering under the closed lids, "I'll sell the land and leave the money to her," he murmured and a tear slid down his cheek. "She should find a man down in the valley, one like what I used to be," he sobbed. He

187

was whimpering in a screechy, stifling voice, his wife came out of the house and asked what was wrong; without looking up he threw the stick at her and kept sobbing inconsolably.

In the evening the brothers returned without the wounded one; he'd been retained at the hospital. Over dinner the father stared at them gloomily, nobody dared speak up. The old man was downing one glass of brandy after another, his bloodshot eyes staring vacantly from his dead-pale face. The space before his eyes was dissolving; all he saw was a heavy undulation of air with indiscernible pieces of furniture and faces floating through it. He circled above his head with his hand, he wanted to brush away the images he was seeing, the mass of dissolved, interchanging faces. Their silence was driving him crazy, he thought he was yelling at them and they didn't talk back, yet in fact he was silent; everything blended in his head, the past and the present, illusion and reality, shapes and emptiness. "I'm going to Australia tomorrow," he gurgled drunkenly, belched and pushed himself away from the table; the chair hurtled to the wall, the metal hit the wood with a clink, and his head jerked as he hit the shelf. He felt a tiny, sharp pain in the temple, as if somebody was threading a needle through his head, he felt the moist wet pain under the scalp, it seemed to him that his brain and eyes were being filled with blood.

In the morning he didn't wake up. They left him in bed until lunch, and when the wife tried to put him in the chair she realised he was dead. She went to the kitchen and told the others. They were silent, staring at her vacantly, only the daughter had tears in her eyes.

"Did he tell you?" the eldest finally asked.

"What?" asked the mother.

"Where he'd buried the gold."

She looked at the empty, tense, hostile faces of her sons. No, he didn't tell her.

"He told me. When you get rid of the neighbour, I'll show you," she said quietly and stubbornly.

"Yes, he's responsible for the old man's death," said the eldest.

"Yes," somebody said, "now we have no choice."

"Yes," somebody said, "we must kill him."

"I'll kill him," somebody said.

"No, we'll kill him together," said the eldest.

"Yes, you have to do it together," said the mother. "You have to do it for father."

The father was buried the following day. It was raining ceaselessly and the roads were flooded with dirty brown streams.

"Now you'll listen to me," said the eldest brother, when they got home covered in mud.

"No, until you get rid of the neighbour and dig out the gold you'll listen to me," said the mother.

"Yes, we'll listen to her," somebody else said.

"He's right, we'll listen to her," said the others.

The coming days one of the brothers was always watching the neighbour's house through the binoculars. For a few days he didn't come out, they assumed that he'd gone into the valley, that he'd fled, but they didn't dare cross over to his farm, they only shot at his dogs from afar. Then one day he emerged before the house, walked about all bent over, he was weak, he'd spent more than a week in bed; once a day he threw some food to the dogs through the window and in the evening milked the cows so that their udders wouldn't burst. His face was covered in blue-green bruises, his ribs still hurt, and daylight irritated his eyes. "I should go down to the valley for food," he thought, but he had no car and was too weak to ride. He knew the neighbours were watching him, he felt their hostile, dim eyes on his body; he wasn't afraid, he just felt sorry that he couldn't live differently. He couldn't leave the homestead of his parents, and although he sometimes considered selling it and moving away, he didn't want to do it; he was too attached to his farm in the embrace of the mountains, to the silent graves of his parents at the forest edge, to the freedom restricted by the violence of the neighbours. After all that had happened he couldn't give up. He was sure the brothers were responsible for his father's death; he was taking his revenge by not giving in. A bullet hit the metal part of his house, he wasn't upset, he knew they were only teasing, they didn't dare kill him just like that, they'd once more try to stage a dirty little accident like a fire or a fall off the horse. He put some lime in the bucket and slowly walked towards the forest dividing the two farms; the two killed dogs were decaying under their fur, giving off a putrid stench, a swarm of flies circled above them; he sprinkled them with lime and spoke out their names into their deaf, decaying hairy ears.

She was watching him through a pair of binoculars, his broad face sunken in, the skin between his strong cheeks and the chin sagging, his shoulders stooping. He was sprinkling the lime powder onto the dogs like a sower sowing seeds into the ground, she felt something warm while watching him, she was no longer sorry she'd covered him up that night. For the first time after the father's death she thought she'd definitely leave the farm one day; this world suddenly wasn't her world any more, the brothers had started fighting among themselves, they were drinking almost every night and the mother could hardly restrain them. It also seemed to her that the eldest brother had started stalking her like a woman, and she felt sick at the thought that he could actually do something to her; she'd kill herself first, she'd kill him first.

During the night she put some bread, cheese and noodles into a black plastic bag, and took it secretely to the neighbour's fence. He heard the barking of his dogs, took the gun and stepped to the window. The dogs kept barking fiercely for a while, then they went quiet. He stared fixedly into the night, checked if the switch for the wired fence was on, turned on the flashlight and scanned the estate; there was nothing unusual to be seen, so he went back to bed and took the gun with him.

In the morning he saw a torn up black plastic bag by the fence. "They've thrown the poison again," he thought. He looked around, but none of his dogs seemed to be in pain, they came running towards him as usual with their tails up. He stepped to the bag and with the tip of his shoe poked out the noodles, cheese and remains of the bread, picked the things up and took them into the house. He didn't know what it meant, "they won't get me so easily," he said and threw the food into the bin.

The following night at more or less the same time he again heard the barking, took the gun and crept to the fence, but saw nobody; only a black bag filled with food was lying on the ground. He dragged it into the house and left it in the hall.

"Somebody went out at night," the eldest brother said in the morning when they started off towards the forest.

"It wasn't me," somebody said.

"Me neither," somebody said.

"It wasn't any of us," somebody said.

"Who was it then?" asked the eldest.

"We don't know," somebody said.

The following day he was strong enough to run the tractor to the field; suspense hung in the air as if before a storm, the birds were flying low and the livestock kept to the shed. He knew he was being watched; the gun was in his pocket. He wasn't afraid of them, he wasn't afraid of anybody, he'd come to terms with the fact that he could be shot down any instant, but he didn't want to live in fear, it was too late to give up. He had hardly started working when the air trembled with a muffled thunder, it seemed as if the mountains would collapse and bury him underneath, it started to pour, but stopped minutes later just as suddenly as it had started. He worked in the field till evening, his body still ached, but he felt he had got out of it well, his body was strong, used to hardship and blows, it was stronger than him.

At night he took the gun, switched off the current in the wiring and crept to the fence. He slid through and hid in the forest. The neighbours' house was dark; he looked intently into the motionless night for almost an hour. He was about to return when he noticed somebody descending down the hill of the neighbouring estate. He took cover and watched the gentle silent steps of the young woman. She came near his fence, the dogs started barking, she threw the bag across and turned round. He dropped the gun and blocked her way. She was frightened and wanted to run away, but he took hold of her hand. She screamed and tried to break free. He didn't let go, he put his arm round her waist, she resisted, grabbed him by the neck and they both fell over. He felt a piercing pain in the ribs, they rolled in the leaves, her firm, soft body was strong, he could hardly restrain her. He held her hands down, pressed her to the ground with his aching chest and fixed her legs with his. She was breathing deeply, her deep eyes stared fixedly into his, her wet lips glistened in the moonlight, her soft breasts made him soft. She was panting wildly and devotedly, closed her eyes, let her head drop back and pushed the tongue out of her mouth. He slowly lowered his mouth towards hers and touched her tongue with his lips. With tiny crackling kisses he went across her face, she was soft and willing, she was giving her warm body to him, she loved and hated the man on top of her, she didn't want to resist; with sharp, muffled sighs she interrupted the silence as he was undressing her. The dogs by the fence were barking fiercely at their struggle, at her panting; sweat gathered on their skin in the meagre light of the moon.

192

First one shot cut though the warm spring night, and then there were blows from all sides. The trees suddenly trembled, the air filled with the thick whirling murmur of the leaves, the smell of decaying animals and rotten roots shot from the soil, the stars dissolved into huge melting yellow carpets. He was sliding down the funnel of white light sucking his body in. He felt her strong embrace, he saw a smile on her lips, the thin cord of life trembled in the air; they remained motionless in a puddle of blood.

Translated by Lili Potpara

Vlado Žabot

Vlado Žabot, born in 1958, studied Slovene and comparative literature at the University of Ljubljana and worked briefly as a journalist. After the publication of his short story collection Bukovska mati (The Book Mother) and novel Stari Pil (Old Pil) he became a freelance writer. Since 2003 he is President of the Slovene Writers' Association. For his work he has received a number of prestigious awards (Prešeren Fund Award, Best Novel of the Year Award, Kajuh Award). His other novels are Pastorala (A Pastoral, translated into Macedonian), Volčje noči (Wolf Nights, translated into German), Nimfa (Nymph), and Sukub (Succubus, translated into English). Since 1985 he has participated successfully in many larger cultural projects; among other things he was the initiator and chief advocate for the introduction of library loan compensation for Slovene authors.

THE SUCCUBUS
(excerpts)

Vlado Žabot

9

He was tempted to confide in his wife. But he was gripped, paralyzed, by the miserable fear that he would just make a fool of himself, humiliate himself, and anyway, she would be neither able nor willing to understand. So all through lunch and through the long afternoon, he kept his thoughts to himself, mulling things over and feeling lost, as if stuck in some horrible sticky ooze in which nothing was certain, nothing gave comfort, while his nervously talkative wife prattled on and on, getting herself all worked up over one thing or another. There was a moment when he just wanted to ram his fist in her mouth, right out of the blue, and yell at her to shut up since this was no ordinary force they had to deal with …

It was precisely this idea that had seized his heart. It lay there like a chilling shadow cast by a dark and swollen cloud. It pressed down on him, making his forehead bead with sweat and stopping his breath, as if he were terrified of the lightning flashes it contained.

197

She noticed nothing of this. She was rambling on about some TV show or something, about someone who had very nicely told or advised the police commander, the captain, that an apartment like this should be protected, sealed off, since that's the proper thing to do, since we were none of us born yesterday and property is, after all, worth something.

He should enlighten her. He should let her know there was much more going on here than it seemed, that the commander only appeared to be a commander, and the captain, too, was not really a captain, and that the whole thing, with all these different disguises and appearances, was nothing but a fraud. But he knew she wouldn't listen to him, that somewhere at some point they had both lost their way, had lost each other. She was already too far away. Too much distance, too much strangeness, had come between them. There were too many mundane truths that were not really true, and now, in the midst of all these seeming truths, they might never again find each another. Might never again find themselves. It was as if some silent, insidious shadow had fallen across their souls ... She was still talking – as if afraid of silence. Among other things, she said that "Mr." Mario had telephoned. That he wanted something from him, from Valent, and had said it was urgent. Valent made no reply when she asked him what business he might possibly have with "Mr." Mario. He just kept on looking at the puffs of smoke and the slightly violet haze hanging over the city, and he just kept on thinking his thoughts, which glowed with a dim light, as if trapped in some thick, sticky substance, with only an occasional bit of clarity, but this too could be just a hallucination. It was impossible to verify. Nothing could be proved for sure. He would like to go back and see how that little girl was ... But this could be exactly what they expected, since probably they knew that he was tormented by uncertainty, which made whatever thought he might have seem illogical, and therefore idiotic, senseless, and pointless.

His wife had at last stopped talking; she seemed simply to have run out of voice. But she hadn't left the bedroom. Even so, Valent was still trying to focus his thoughts on the puffs of smoke and all the hundreds of cattle that were needed every day to supply the city's daily meal, but such thoughts could not drown out the muffled noise of scraping, from end to end, along the wall, as if someone in the Kremavc apartment was secretly, but very persistently, drawing a line. He felt a slight quivering in his stomach or somewhere thereabouts. Something was also going on with his lips and facial expression, all of which had to be coaxed into a more or less convincing display of self-composure.

"It's all nonsense, Olga," he said, shaking his head, as if the main thing he wanted was to reassure her. He also tried to lower his voice somewhat, to make it sound soothing and soft. He walked over to the wall. And after listening intently a few moments, he again shook his head. And shrugged. Then, as if he thought he might possibly have heard some sort of rustling overhead, he looked up at the ceiling. Actually, it seemed to him that the best thing would be to speak out, as it were, in defense of his own position in the house, to remind his wife, in meaningfully raised tones, that he very much regretted her inability to stand by his side as a wife should, by which he meant that there was nothing they both could believe in together – and that the answers, even if one believed in them, simply did not exist … Of course, they could still inspire sufficient courage so a person did not lose his dignity when, for instance, people suspected him of murder, that is to say, of one of the many murders that, to be sure, happen every day and go on happening and which, like the days themselves, are lost in oblivion. He would also like to tell her about the Shalimar and the little girl, and to stress the possibility that, for now, they might just be tailing him, observing him through this or that wall, which very likely meant they could come for him at any moment. They would probably have done so already, of course, if they did not have other purposes in mind. Other purposes! – he would say emphatically – other purposes! And maybe he would even raise his index finger to underscore the point. Maybe she would only look at him in amazement. And maybe she would finally understand that he was not just anybody, that is to say, not just one of her soap-opera characters, and the main thing was that he knew what it meant that they had not yet taken him away. Ah, these purposes! – he'd repeat, again with suitable emphasis. These purposes, my dear! That is what it's all about – this scratching on the wall, this perfumed letter and Mario, and certainly the captain, too, many such captains, many such Marios, and other people, too, and other things we don't need to ask about right now – it's all part of these purposes. Of course, were he to raise his voice like this and explain the whole thing, she might only feel worse. So for her own sake, for her own good, it was better to say nothing. And she would probably not believe it anyway, even if very early in the morning he were to show her the "mountain."

"And that's another problem," he said, a little carried away.

She was looking at him as if something in his face was starting to make her afraid.

"That is to say" – he was getting confused – "a problem, yes, I'd say it's a problem if you don't believe me."

Obviously she didn't understand.

But that was hardly important.

"You're strange," she could not help saying.

"We're all strange, Olga . . ."

"Valent!"

"Well, that's what I think."

"Something is not right with you, mister."

"Heh, heh, heh." He opened his mouth a little more than he needed to. And showed her his teeth. And looked up at the ceiling. And then back at her. And of course he would have kept on doing this, over and over, but she stormed out of the bedroom as if something had stung her in the butt.

"You'll hear the sounds, too, yes, you will! Heh, heh! Why shouldn't you?" he muttered to himself in a kind of jeer, then went back to the window and thought how she would be reaching for her strongest tranquilizers right about now. And how all those herds of cattle were disappearing into the city's gullet every day, and how this thought wouldn't get anyone anywhere.

"That's true," he agreed, half-aloud. "It won't get anyone anywhere … Because we are all trapped. Heh, heh. Because you are trapped, too, wifey dear!" He said it loud enough for her to hear him – and then to himself alone: "And because they are trapped, too."

"You have a telephone call." He had not heard her come back to the bedroom. He thought she must have taken an extra dose of tranquilizers; she looked contrite and walked and talked as if in the presence of a corpse. When he did not immediately turn away from the window, she mumbled something about him being deaf; of course she did not understand that he could care less about the telephone and that whoever it was who wanted something from him could just wait a moment. He did not move until she again, now in a much louder voice, reminded him that he had a call; then he went to the phone and said, slowly, in a low drawl, "Hello." As soon as he heard the voice of "Mr." Mario, his heart sank. "Kosmina?!" The man had the gall to address him in this impudent way. It sounded like a warning. "Tonight, at 12:37, be in Gustav Kremavc's apartment." And that was all. Just like that. Without so much as a by-your-leave. Twelve-thirty-seven. And then this so-called "gentleman" simply hung up the phone. How do you like that? The guy just hung up. No explanation. No anything. And now his wife was already in the doorway, watching him as he tried to make sense of the dead air on the other end of the line and then, frustrated, fairly slammed down the receiver.

"What'd she want?" she asked, with covert but firm determination in her voice, as if to demand an explanation, as if the phone call had something to do with her or was even mainly about her.

"What do you mean, 'she'? This was ..." He didn't understand. Embarrassed, he looked away. And in fact, he had no idea what to say.

"Who was that little girl, Valent?" Obviously, she had not mistaken his embarrassment. And he couldn't say he was just playing games. But if he tried to explain it by telling her that maybe, indeed, some little girl had made the phone call but that it was undoubtedly "Mr." Mario who then got on the line and continued the conversation, there would still be the difficult question of what it was, in fact, that this Mario person all of a sudden wanted.

"This fellow you like so much," he started to explain, as if he'd just had enough of it all. "This Mario, or whatever he's called – he's looking for a new job" – he had come up with something now – "and he's been pestering me to put in a good word for him somewhere." He tried to indicate to her, both in his voice and with his eyes, that at least as far as he was concerned, this conversation was over. But that worked only for a second, during which he heard a line being scratched across the wall.

"The little girl who called wanted to talk to you herself," she continued, not taking her eyes off him. She spoke in a low tone, as if she didn't want the neighbors to hear, but at the same time, the obvious tension in her voice told him she wouldn't put up with any games on his part.

"But it was just Mario . . ." He was trying to make a joke of it all the same, as if he were sorry that "little girl" hadn't been more persistent.

"Oh really?" she said, with an even icier stare. "Mr. Mario is certainly not looking for any job."

He just shrugged his shoulders as if there were no point in even laughing about it.

10

His thoughts were like a heavy burden that had piled up from god knows where. They came one after another, all in a tangle, in bits and pieces or stretched into some miserable, unrecognizable, incomprehensible mass, and for the most part they were all just useless. Barren. In fact, they were commonplace, everyday thoughts, the kind everyone knows, secondhand, threadbare, many already discarded – and none of them got him anywhere or gave him any answers. Mainly, what all this stuff in his head did was make him feel restless, with a nightmarish feeling of being in a hurry, like flashes and sparks crackling above an unseen fire someone kept poking at, flaming up and dying down and meaning absolutely nothing, nothing you could grasp or understand, since it was simply impossible for a person to find his way in such circumstances, since life and the city and everything else seemed both cheap and harrowing at the same time, since he didn't know how or with what or to what end he might make sense of anything, since all of it together was giving him the shakes and the only thing he could do was wish it would somehow just all be over, one way or another. He had the feeling that all this stuff, bit by bit and sometimes distorted beyond recognition, from the street and the buildings and the people, was taking him over, all of this rushing about, all these sounds from the television set, all this pointlessness, insignificance, worthlessness, which all the same demanded its daily meal every single day, all these appearances and guises, which in fact were forms of despair and bewilderment and confusion; and meanwhile maybe someone jumps or falls or screams, and of course it hardly mattered if one or another person died, if one or another person missed somebody or killed somebody, since all the while on television they just kept on doing what they do and no one was the wiser, neither here nor there nor anywhere. It was precisely at this point, perhaps, that it hardly mattered if you were this or that thing – if for instance you were a goat, or maybe an ant; it hardly mattered if you believed this thing or that thing or didn't believe it; what was important was that the daily meal got served and nothing got muddled, that for instance all the cars and streetcars and trains didn't collide in one big pile-up, and that everything somehow seemed to run smoothly, so your wife could take her daily dose of tranquilizers and watch the different actors on television chase each other, cheat on each other, stab each other, or discuss healthy and unhealthy diets and diet supplements, which were part of the whole thing and had a positive influence on your sense of well-being. The whole thing, yes. And at the same time you begin to suspect that you are, in a little way, part of the whole thing and that in fact there is nothing else. Fine, you tell yourself, the names will stay – but you also know that there are, or rather, will be later, more and more of them every day and that soon there will be entirely too many. And the whole thing is saturated with sounds – it rumbles and vibrates – and meanwhile the evening passes slowly … and this line that was being scratched across the wall of the Kremavc apartment seems at some point to have stopped – and now there are only muffled, furtive rustling noises coming from over there, which catch your attention every so often through the sounds of the television.

It was after eleven. His wife had fallen asleep. But Valent still had no idea what to do; he just kept moving about, changing his seat and pacing through the apartment, then he would, repeatedly, stand in front of the window and, through his own reflected outline in the glass, let his gaze wander across the arrays of lights in the eastern districts, and he did not, in fact, know what to do with all these thoughts. He was sorry he had not simply gone to Brežine, where, with a glass of burgundy and a well-stoked pipe, things might not seem quite so strange and obtrusive and where he might have been able to simply forget about that "little girl" – and "Mr." Mario, too. But it was too late now. And, presumably, somebody was already there waiting for him in his deceased neighbor's apartment … He tamped his pipe and lit it, then tried to settle into that slightly absent feeling of elation, of losing himself in the smoke, which was usually so agreeable – but now there was only a burning in his mouth, as if he had scorched it, and the saliva that gathered there was insipid and watery; it was really just spit, and he had to keep swallowing it over and over, with a feeling of disgust.

Then his wife woke up with a sudden jolt and, in a kind of distracted bewilderment, sat up on the couch. She looked here and there and clearly did not know what she was looking at or why; and for a brief moment her eyes rested on him, too, but then, as if he were not the thing she wanted – that is, nothing special, of no particular interest – she just stood up and went into the bedroom. Just like that, without a word. It must be the drugs, he thought; she was more or less always stoned, and the two of them had become strangers … and he would just let them wait, whoever was there in Kremavc's apartment, if, of course, he decided to go at all, if he decided, in fact, to pay any attention to them whatsoever … and maybe whatever was now about to happen had already been decided, who knows how or why, and all other possibilities were actually just a cover … and meanwhile people kept pushing and shoving, as if by some divinely spiteful decree, and they could care less about all these different names (who knows whose?) that day in, day out, dissolve into oblivion like smoke. But he had no idea what it was all about – or what this pain was, pressing in his chest.

He had poured himself a glass of cognac and drunk it.

It hadn't helped.

Nor, later, did a second glass. On television people were still chasing each other and beating each other up. His mouth still tasted watery, insipid – and now a certain doubt, a certain suspicion, was aroused … he was, after all, well aware of the fact that there was no one he could trust, no one who'd stand by his side in the present situation. His two sons would tell him some nonsense about how he was imagining it all and that he should just try to get some rest. There was no point in going to the building manager or the police. If he tried phoning someone, whoever was in the Kremavc apartment would hear him and then of course just slip away or disappear before they got there.

A little before 12:30 he turned off the TV, shook out his pipe, and listened intently. There was only silence. From down below a muffled hum stretched across the city. Everyone in the apartment tower was probably already asleep. He couldn't even hear his wife's breathing. There was, indeed, a ringing in his ears, and every so often his heart seemed to founder a bit, and he had to control his breathing – but not the slightest sign of life could be heard from the Kremavc place. He even went up to the wall and pressed his ear against it. Nothing was moving. There wasn't the smallest sound. So the dead are all silence, he thought, and this hidden terror lying dormant in man is pure nonsense. And all this stuff about the Kremavc apartment was just a bad joke meant to confuse him and rob him of sleep. Which of course he wouldn't allow. Would definitely not let happen. First, he would go to bed. And then, he would maybe try to make himself believe in coincidences, that is to say, in the zero at the end of the equation, that is, in the

206

zero on the right and left sides of the equal sign, and that all this stuff piling up everywhere from every side was nothing but a cover for nothingness, zero-ness.

So he had made up his mind …

But when he came out of the bathroom and turned off the lights, the telephone rang.

Long, horrible, sharp, it cut into the silence – but at the same time it seemed somehow far away. Afraid mainly that the ringing might wake his wife, but also because of this weirdly annoying faraway sound in the ring, he ran into the front hall and simply unplugged the phone. And in the same moment, without clearly thinking about it, as if he were absolutely sure he'd find someone lurking outside, he unlocked the door and peered into the hallway.

There was only dense and silent darkness.

Nevertheless, though already in his pajamas, he stepped over to the Kremavc apartment and, without hesitation, knocked firmly, resolutely, on the door. But the door, which must not have been fully closed, yielded to his knock and opened a little, which he hadn't at all expected. Still, he managed to control his nerves, at least enough to call out, in a low but fairly strong voice and with apparent self-assurance, through the partially opened door into the dark, hollow silence: "Good evening."

No one answered.

He thought he smelled the sweet scent of Shalimar. But the next moment he was not entirely sure about this.

He called out a second time.

"Is anyone there?" he added after a pause.

It occurred to him that he should not go in there alone, that is, not without witnesses; that it could all be a trap they were trying to lure him into so they could then accuse him of robbery or burglary, or something worse.

"It's … Kosmina here," he said in a much lower voice, standing in the doorway – just to be sure all the same. Then,

207

listening intently, he waited a little. Finally, after some time had gone by, he pressed the doorbell. It didn't work. It had never before occurred to him that these meal-service agencies might be just a front, that their so-called delivery people, who came into daily contact with elderly pensioners, knew precisely what was going on with every one of their subscribers. But now he was almost convinced that whenever the opportunity presented itself, whenever one of their, ideally, solitary subscribers died, they would just come right into his apartment – maybe even in collusion with the building manager – and take whatever was most valuable, and then if need be, just to be on the safe side, they could use various tried and true ploys to cast suspicion on some naïve neighbor. In any case, he felt he was right not to enter the Kremavc apartment. He had not taken the bait. After all, it would be hard to explain later what he had been looking for in the middle of the night in his late neighbor's unsealed apartment. The best thing, he thought, would be to recruit some other neighbor as a witness and then go tell the building manager. But unfortunately, he did not have many close, or even particularly friendly, contacts with any of his neighbors. But that wasn't important now. So he switched on the hallway light and went to the nearest door – the nameplate said "Vidic-Gross" – and rang the doorbell. But he had to ring it twice, and then a third time, and was already losing patience when finally he heard a noise in the apartment and then a woman angrily asking who was out there and what did he want. Looking through the peephole, she asked him if he had any idea what time it was, and then, in a louder voice, said that she would not allow this sort of –

"Madam," he interrupted her in his low Brežine drawl, "this is a serious matter." And then he asked if her husband was at home.

It was none of his business, she said.

"Please listen to me, madam," he nevertheless continued in a rather dignified, polite tone. "It looks as though somebody has

208

broken into our neighbor's apartment …" But she was obviously in a foul mood and wouldn't let him finish. What went on in someone else's apartment was none of her concern, all she wanted was some peace and quiet in the middle of the night …

"That's fine, madam," he broke in, trying to calm her down. "I just thought that if it were possible …"

"Why don't you call the police?" She didn't want to listen to him. "If you don't, I will, and I'm doing it right now too," she said, as if to threaten him, from somewhere deeper inside the apartment. And from the sound of it, she had in fact begun to call the police.

That was fine with him. The police would have to be called anyway, eventually. But first, all the same, he wanted someone as a witness. So skipping two or three doors without any nameplates, he went straight over to the apartment of a retired watchmaker named Marzi; he had once had coffee and a cognac with this fellow and ever since they would always greet each other with a nod. He rang the doorbell and at the same time called out for Mr. Marzi in a resolute tone that was, perhaps, loud enough to be heard in one of the other occupied apartments on the floor.

This time he didn't have to wait long.

And after looking through the peephole to see who it was, Mr. Marzi even opened the door.

"Oh my god, someone broke in, you say?" he said, alarmed and amazed after Valent told him in a few words about Kremavc and the open door. Then he looked over toward the Kremavc apartment.

"I wonder if you would also take a look …"

"Yes, of course, of course." He was so upset he could hardly get the words out. And now Mrs. Marzi, too, was at the door. Pale and trying to arrange her rather disheveled hair, she at once asked what was wrong.

"He says someone broke into the Kremavc apartment," her husband explained in a hushed and somewhat confiding tone. Mrs. Marzi likewise immediately glanced toward Kremavc's door and then, with a rather stern appraising eye, took a good look at Valent.

"A lady in another apartment," Valent looked down the hall-way, "Mrs. Vidic-Gross, has probably already called the police."

"Oh dear god!" Marzi was still quite upset and kept shaking his head and looking around. His wife meanwhile, her arms crossed over her breasts, was eyeing Valent as if she had certain reservations.

"Even this morning I heard someone walking around in there, scratching on the wall . . ."

"Really?" Marzi looked at him meaningfully from beneath his high, bald scalp, which had just a little bit of hair over the ears.

"Oleti should be told, too . . ."

"Oh, well, that Oleti fellow . . ." Marzi said dismissively of the building manager, speaking in a hesitant, muffled tone.

"And again this evening I heard a kind of shuffling sound ..."

"So someone must have broken in," Marzi volunteered the obvious conclusion and once more looked over toward the Kremavc place. But by now Mrs. Marzi had already started down the hall, and the other two followed.

Valent wondered a moment whether he should try to per-suade the Marzis to go in with him, all three of them together, and look around the apartment, but then he decided it would be best if one of them suggested this.

But the door to the Kremavc apartment was shut tight.

Locked. As Mrs. Marzi had discovered.

Still, Valent needed to make sure for himself and so pressed down hard on the door handle – since, really, it was incredible, and very aggravating, too, of course; it put him in a very awkward position, as the three of them exchanged looks and he did all he could to maintain the composure of a self-assured and thoroughly respectable man.

"Yes, it seems that …" – Marzi had bent down to the keyhole and was examining it closely from all angles – "it doesn't really look as if … No, I wouldn't say the lock has been tampered with."

Valent did his best not to appear ridiculous as he felt Mrs. Marzi's eyes on him, but he had no idea what to think or say that might be even a little helpful.

Marzi got up from the keyhole and, still looking at it, gave a shrug.

"It was definitely open earlier," Valent insisted. But now, even to himself, he seemed less than convincing and not at all Brežine-like. Mrs. Marzi was watching him from the corner of her eye.

"If it *had* been broken into …" Marzi said, still shaking his head at the keyhole.

"Wait a second," Valent whispered; he'd worked it out now. Meaningfully, he placed a hand on Marzi's shoulder. "They're probably still in there."

Marzi looked first at Valent and then at his wife. She, evidently, had her doubts about Valent's supposition.

"You think they locked themselves inside?" Marzi, too, seemed doubtful now.

"Yes, I do." He saw no need to conceal his disappointment with the rather insulting second thoughts they seemed to be having. It was true he hadn't checked before to see if the apartment had literally been broken into, and that was how he had described the situation to them – but he certainly had no intention of going into any of this now. A little impatiently, as if wondering why it was taking the police so long to get there, he looked back down the hall to the elevator and then a moment later, with a measure of haughty disdain, looked straight into Mrs. Marzi's eyes. Which at least she appeared to take in stride. She even let out a yawn.

"Well then, so now …" Marzi sighed with a shrug, mainly, it seemed, out of consideration for Valent, but he obviously had no idea what to say.

"We wait for the police to get here," Valent said in a low but determined voice.

"Yes, of course." Marzi was not entirely sure. But he evidently thought it best to keep his reservations to himself. In the meantime, Mrs. Marzi had stepped right up to the door and with a finger to her lips indicated to the two men that she thought she might have heard something. All three held their breath.

Quite a bit of time passed before Mrs. Marzi finally shook her head in disgust, stepped back from the door, and said she, for one, didn't believe there was anyone in there.

"What if we …" Marzi once more began but didn't finish.

"They're laying low," Valent whispered.

Again, the three of them were silent. And as if embarrassed, they avoided each other's eyes. Then all of them, in unison, turned to look at the elevator as it started to rumble. But apparently it was stopping on one of the lower floors.

And then, a little while later, it went up to one of the higher floors.

"The door *was* open," Valent said, breaking the silence in a low, confidential voice. He sensed that the Marzis lacked the will to keep this hallway vigil up for long. "Then I went over to that other apartment" – he nodded toward the Vidic-Gross place – "but I never once let this door out of my sight." This wasn't entirely true, since Mrs. Vidic-Gross's foul mood had caused him to forget, briefly, about the open door, and then later, while he was going down the hallway – that is, to the Marzis' – he did not exactly keep his eye on the Kremavc apartment the whole time. But he was sure he would have heard something if someone had meanwhile slipped out of the apartment, especially if they had locked the door behind them.

Still, the stairs and the elevator were not very far away, just seven or eight steps at most. But he really saw no reason to doubt his supposition that the door had been locked from the inside. Of course, his suspicions fell on "Mr." Mario and, more and more, on the building manager, too. But for now he felt it best not to mention any of this.

When after a really unconscionable length of time the police had still not appeared, he realized that Mrs. Vidic-Gross had never telephoned them at all. So he suggested that perhaps Mrs. Marzi should phone the police and, naturally, demand an explanation for why they were taking so long to get here.

But she replied that it would be better for Valent to call them himself since he could more easily describe what had happened; she wouldn't know what to say, after all, and anyway, as far as she was concerned, the best thing would be for them all to just go back to bed.

But she stayed there all the same, though it seemed, at least on the surface, that she wasn't very happy about it.

"I had thought it might be better if your husband and I stayed here by the door," Valent tried to explain amicably. "Who knows, they might try to make a run for it."

"Oh, for god's sake!" She no longer saw any need for whispering. "There's no one in there!"

"What about Oleti?" Now Marzi was trying to be amicable.

"I think," Valent whispered, leaning toward him and gesturing with his thumb toward the door, "that it's Oleti who's in there."

This made an impression on Marzi, or at least it seemed that way. He even nodded as if he understood and agreed. But the next moment he looked again at his wife, and in their quick exchange of glances Valent could detect something like a hint of mockery. This stung him, but it also made him more determined to make that telephone call. To prove them wrong and wipe these mocking looks off their faces. And so without saying another word but inwardly fuming, he hurried back to his own apartment with long and resolute steps.

But on entering his front hall, out of the corner of his eye he caught a glimpse of the girl, just as she was slipping off into the living room.

He was stunned; for a second he even thought he was going to faint …

He remembered the appointment, of course, and the letter, this "seal upon your heart," and thought that maybe, looking at it all together, it was not actually a prank. The rich fragrance of a heady sweet perfume still lingered in the front hall.

His heart was strangely seized with yearning. He had to lean against the wall.

Thoughts crowded in on him all at once. The girl was some-how actually here, but even so – he didn't understand . . . it was happening too fast, there was too much he had to grasp, and all of it at once, and there were all sorts of things he had to work out in his mind . . . He somehow felt annoyed at the girl for being here; it wasn't exactly a pleasant surprise . . . Still, he had no wish to betray her, nor did he want to wake his wife . . . And without thinking it all through, without actually knowing why, he said, as if he were speaking on the telephone, "Hello!" – not into the phone but rather directing his voice back into the hallway through the open door of the apartment. "The door was unlocked. It was open, yes …" he continued. "Mr. Kremavc's apartment, the one who just died … yes, yes, but someone's locked it now … yes, that same apartment … Tomorrow? What do you mean, tomorrow?! But really … None of our business? Why, of course it is! We're his neighbors, after all …" He was surprised how easily the words came to him; he imagined the little girl hiding somewhere in the living room and thought how grateful she must be that he was doing this, and even how she must be admiring the way he was handling the situation.

214

"I'll be back in a second," he whispered toward the living room, as if confiding a secret, and then quickly went back out to the Marzis, who even at a distance were trying to guess from his expression what was going on and how things now stood.

Naturally, he feigned disappointment as he told them in a few words that the police were not coming, or rather, that they would be here but not until tomorrow and that this was supposedly no concern of even the closest neighbors.

The Marzis just looked at each other.

They just stood there unable to decide what to do, and all three of them looked back at the door of the Kremavc apartment, and then down the hallway, and Valent tried, with some difficulty, to conceal his nervousness, his trembling and impatience – his curiosity, in fact, which was pulling him, enticing him back – and he even found it hard to breathe when, with a display of indecision, as if he really had no idea what to do, he began to apologize for disturbing them in the middle of the night, but now, given the views of the police, he didn't think it wise for them to take matters into their own hands.

The other two said nothing.

Marzi pouted his lips and shook his head. Mrs. Marzi, it seemed, was keeping her thoughts to herself; in any case, she offered no comment, or maybe just had nothing to add.

"What do you two think? I really don't know …" Valent said after a pause; all the same, he wanted to hear them say something.

"Hmm . . . How should I know?" Marzi muttered.

"I've said what I have to say." His wife shook her head scornfully. Valent didn't like the way she shook her head. But now he did not have the time, or the desire, to delve into this. He just shrugged his shoulders so as to let them know they could do whatever they felt was best.

"Of course, we could still wait here." He tried to sound convincing. Naturally, he expected Mrs. Marzi, at least, to voice a different opinion. But she didn't. Instead, she asked him if he had called the building manager as well.

He shook his head.

"He thinks, you know … that Oleti might be in on it," Marzi stammered, in a whisper, to his wife.

"Well, I mean, I can't be sure …" Valent said evasively, as if mainly he didn't want to be held accountable. "A person can think one thing or another about such-and-such a matter, but if the police say – I mean, what do I know? – if they're not particularly interested, well, then – you mind your own business and then something happens and suddenly you find yourself in the middle of it all."

"You look a little pale to me, Mr. Kosmina," was Mrs. Marzi's only comment to all this. And Valent felt a somewhat stronger tightening in his chest. Comments like this alarmed him. But still he managed to collect himself enough to make some remark about how late it was, and how we're not getting any younger, and so on, and even to attempt a smile, but he wasn't all that successful. Now Marzi, too, was eyeing him with a rather worried and somewhat pitying look; obviously, he agreed with his wife's assessment.

"I wonder what was wrong with him – Mr. Kremavc, I mean," Mrs. Marzi continued, as if this might have something to do with Valent's paleness. They were both wondering.

"I really don't know," Valent shrugged. There was a note of reluctance in his voice. "After all, one doesn't get involved in other people's affairs, and we actually hardly ever saw each other. And now this happens. I don't know if it makes any sense …" They apparently didn't know, either. So Valent just turned around and took a few steps toward his apartment, and then, as if he had remembered something, turned back to them, shrugged his shoulders, and muttered, as if to himself, that it really made no sense at all. He was getting more and more

216

impatient. He was even afraid someone else might join the three of them here in the hallway and then it would all drag out until morning, which of course would mean that the girl would not be able to leave his apartment without being seen. His wife, of course, would raise hell and a half. And then everyone would know that he had never called the police and who knows what else. Oh, there'd be trouble, all right. Lots of explaining to do. And on top of it all, the little girl would never forgive him.

"Know what? I'm going to bed," he finally told them. He knew the Marzis would look at him strangely and imagine god knows what. "I'm not feeling so well," he added and, with a worried look, shook his head. Then, as if he had done all that a man of honor could and must do, and without paying any attention to their long silent stares, and sensing that he had not succeeded in convincing them and, indeed, had almost certainly aroused their suspicions as to his own behavior, he just walked back to his apartment and shut the door, locking it behind him.

11

But the girl was not to be found. He looked everywhere she might possibly hide, even in the bedroom. She simply seemed to have vanished. And while he was a little relieved at this idea, mainly because of his wife and all the aggravation that might have followed, still he was hardly happy about it ...

Translated by Rawley Grau